CHICAGO CUBS

MOLLIE MARTIN

CREATIVE EDUCATION

A real smasher. Catcher Randy Hundley was injured, but he still led the Chicago Cubs into the season of '72.

Copyright © 1982 by Creative Paperback, Inc. International copyrights reserved in all countries. No part of this book may be reproduced in any form without written permission from the publisher.

Library of Congress Cataloging in Publication Data

Martin, Mollie.
  Chicago Cubs.

  Summary: A history of the baseball team that is the only one of the original eight charter members of the National League that has stayed in business in the same city for more than 100 years.
    1. Chicago Cubs (Baseball team)—History—Juvenile literature.   [1. Chicago Cubs (Baseball team)—History.   2. Baseball—History]
I. Title.
[GV875.C6M37   1982b]   796.357'64'0977311   82-16181
ISBN 0-89812-265-1 (pbk.)

CHICAGO CUBS

WHY "CUBS"? In 1876, Chicago's club was called the "White Stockings." Later, it was called the "Chicagos," then the "Colts" and the "Orphans." Legend has it that a newspaper writer gave the team its permanent nickname, "Cubs," in 1902. He picked the name because it was short and fit well into a newspaper headline.

Centuries ago the fragrance of the wild onions that grew along the south shore of Lake Michigan was so powerful that the Indians who lived near there named the area after that strong smell. They called it, in their own language, "Checagou".

By the year 1837, more than four thousand new settlers made their home along those shores. They adopted the Indian name for their settlements, but Americanized the spelling to "Chicago"

Today, the city of Chicago, Illinois, has a population of more than 3.5 million, the second largest in the United States.

The aroma of the wild onions is long gone, replaced by the exciting sights and sounds of a bustling metropolis. Chicago now is known as "The Windy City" because of the swirling, gusting breezes that blow off Lake Michigan into the city.

Chicago leads all United States cities in the production of hundreds of important products such as steel, saws, bolts and paint that help us put our country together.

Chicago is also known for its professional sports teams: the soccer Sting, the football Bears, the basketball Bulls. The windy City even has two baseball teams, the White Sox of the American League and the Cubs of the National League.

Of all those sports teams, however, one team always seems to rank highest on the Chicago popularity list. It hasn't won more championships than the other teams. It hasn't produced more superstars than other teams. It doesn't even necessarily have the brightest future of all the Chicago teams.

Nevertheless, there's no doubt that the Cubs are Chicago's favorite team. Why? Call it history, heritage or tradition, the team and the fans seem to have a special bond that will carry them through thick and thin. The traditions are long and deep.

In August of '29, the Cubs' leaders were already plotting their World Series strategy. (Left) Joe Burk, coach; Joe McCarthy, manager; and Grover Land, coach.

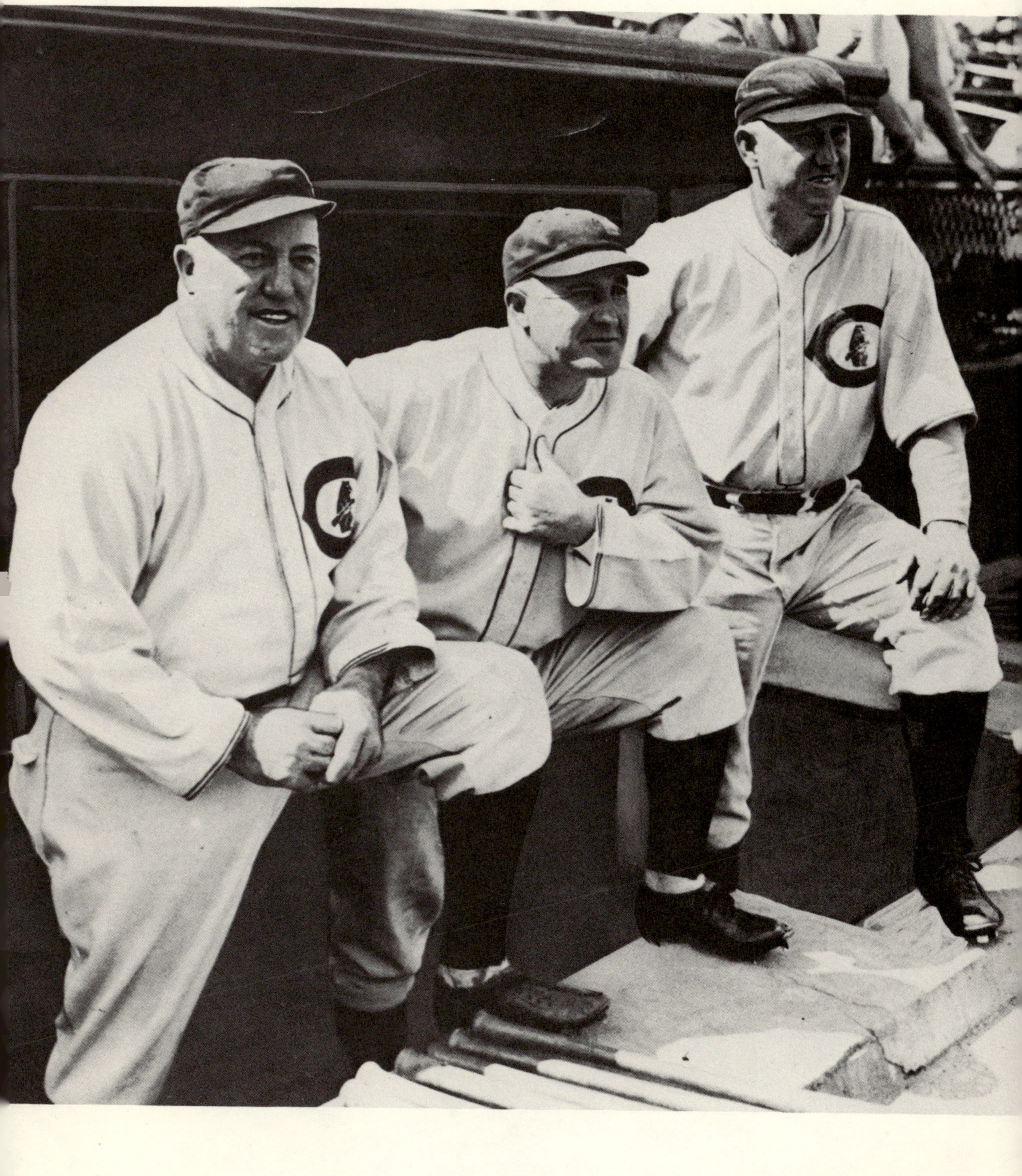

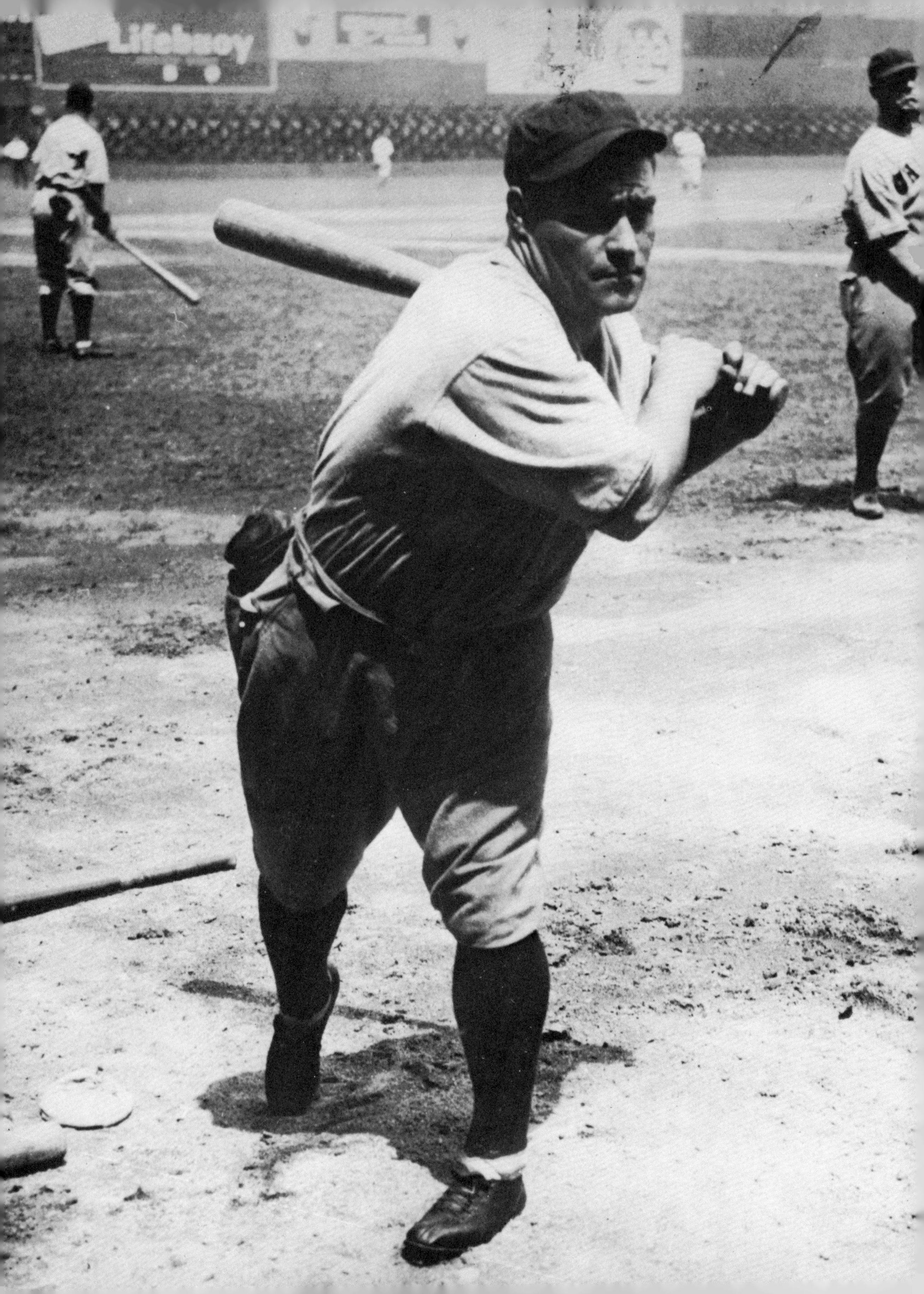
Lifebuoy

- The Cubs are the only one of the original eight charter members of the National League that has stayed in business in the same city for more than 100 years.
- Wrigley Field is the only major-league baseball park that does not have artificial lighting. All games are played during the day, another part of Cubs tradition.
- The Cubs always have taken care of their young fans. The Cubs have given away hundreds of thousands of tickets to Boy Scouts, Little Leaguers and others so that kids can see their favorite team play.

There are lots of other reasons why Chicagoans continue to support the Cubs. Simply put, the Cubs like to win. Over the years they have:
- Won two World Series championships.
- Captured 10 modern National League pennants.
- Seen 30 former players inducted into the Baseball Hall of Fame.
- Had 115 All-Star game selections.
- Watched 23 pitchers win 20 or more games in a single season.
- Racked up ten no-hitters.

The statistics go on and on. But the best thing about Cubs fans is that they don't judge their team only on numbers or win-loss records. It's the people — the fans, the players, the coaches, the executives — who make the Cubs so great.

From the very start, the Cubs' forefathers were as concerned about their fans as they were about the players. That concern helped get the National League — and modern-day baseball — underway.

THE CUBS ARE BORN

William A. Hulbert, a wealthy grain broker, was worried. He owned a baseball club in Chicago, but the

His style at the plate looked awkward, but Hack Wilson terrified enemy pitchers. (1929)

NAME SOUND FAMILIAR? The year the National League began, Albert Spalding won 47 of 60 games, with an earned run average of 1.75. That year he also started a company called A. G. Spalding & Brothers. His company manufactured the National League's first official ball. Today, Spalding is still one of the top names in sporting goods equipment.

BEST BUYS
Two of the Cubs' best player purchases had to be Hack Wilson and Ernie Banks. Chicago got the rights to Wilson in 1925 for $5,000; Wilson went on to hit 56 home runs in 1930. And the Cubs bought the rights to negotiate with Banks.

reputation of the sport was going downhill.

Gambling was out of control. Even the players bet on their own games. Fans players and managers alike didn't hesitate to drink liquor before games. Discipline was so lacking that players would fail to show up for many of the contests. Hulbert feared the repectable fans would stop coming to the ballparks altogether.

Finally, in 1875, he made a decision. He packed his bags and traveled around the country. He met with the owners of the strongest clubs — St. Louis, Cincinnati, Louisville, New York, Hartford, Boston and Philadelphia — and convinced them that baseball needed a league. That's how the National League was born.

Before Chicago played its first game in the new league, Hulbert made sure that he had a good manager. He convinced Albert G. Spalding to leave the Boston club to join his team.

Spalding was also a tremendous pitcher. He shut out Louisville 4-0 in Chicago's first N.L. game. Ross Barnes was the team's slugging champion. With Spalding and Barnes, Chicago (officially called the Chicago National Association Club) would go on to win the National League's very first pennant in 1876.

Hulbert became president of the league in 1877, but died in 1882. So Spalding took over as president of the Chicago club and Adrian Anson became the team's new manager. Behind Anson, Chicago won five more pennants in the seven years between 1880 and 1886.

"CAP ANSON" COMES TO TOWN

Adrian Constantine "CAP" Anson was a pioneer in more than one way. He had the distinction of being the first baby born in the pioneer settlement of Marshalltown, Iowa in 1851.

Anson introduced the game of baseball to the Univer-

Mordecai Brown needed only three good fingers to become one of the National League's poserful hurlers. (1936).

10

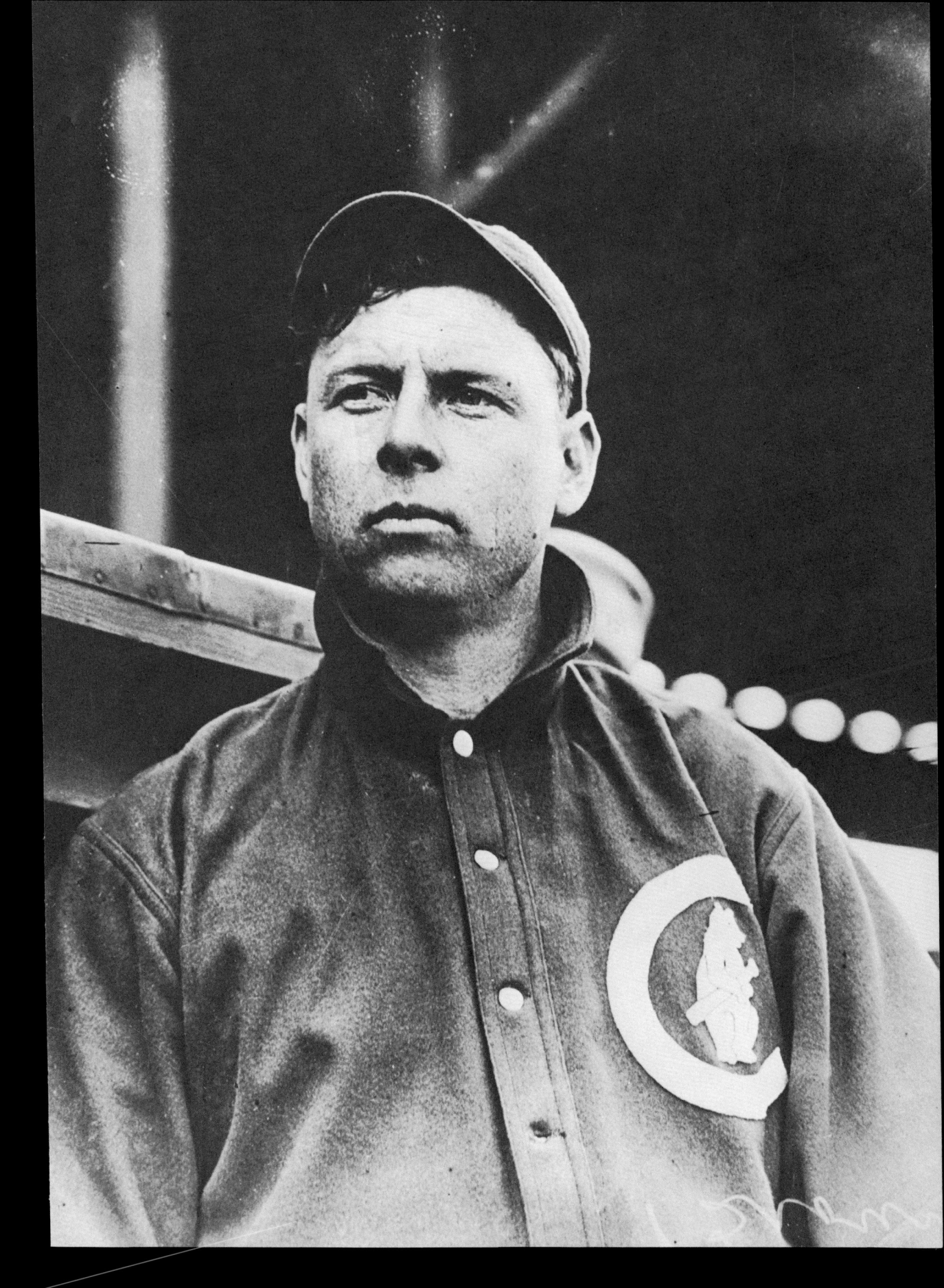

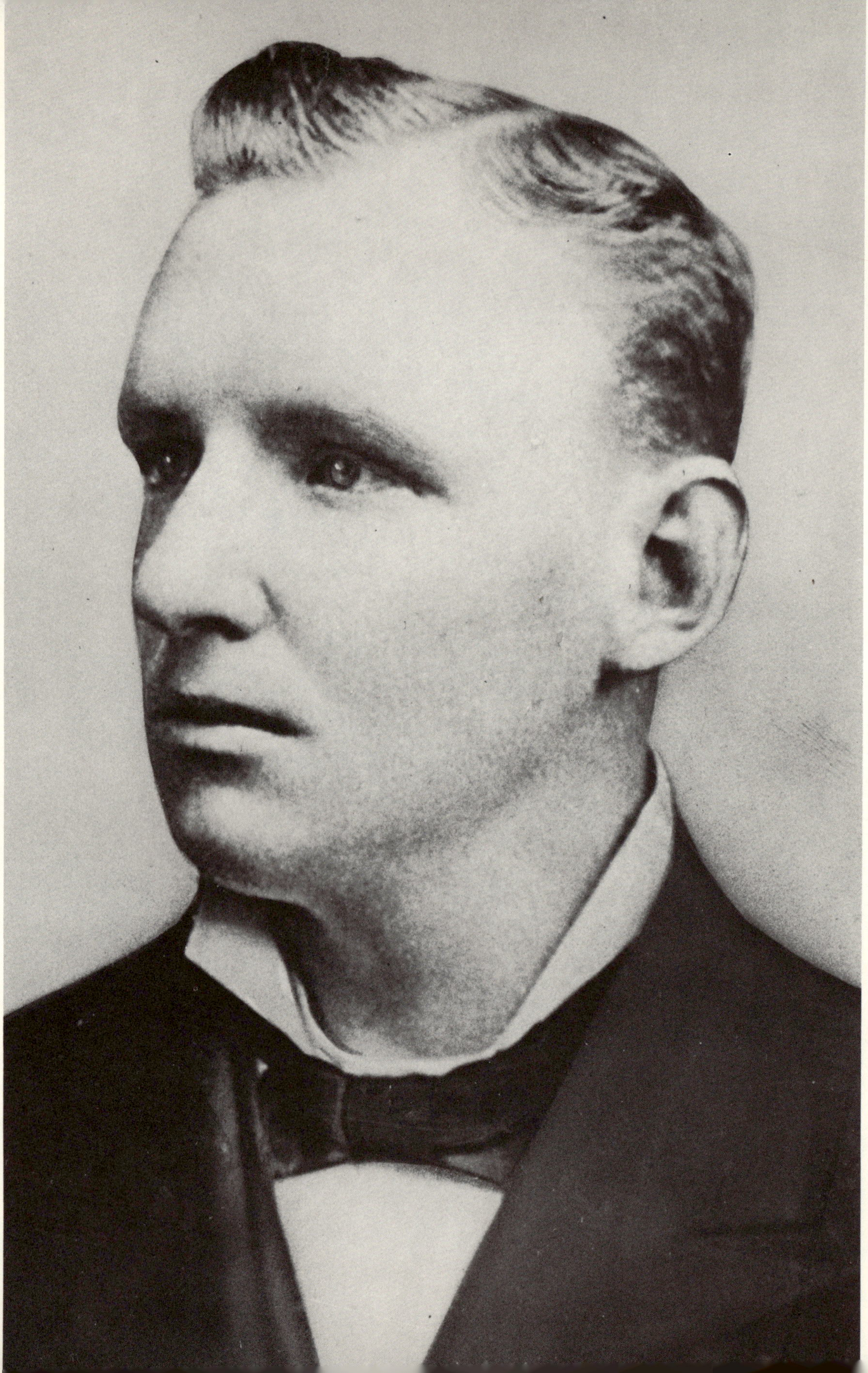

sity of Notre Dame when he was a student there. Then he moved on to the National League. In his first season with Chicago, Anson hit .365. His batting average would be over. 300 in 20 of his 22 seasons with the Cubs!

By the time he retired in 1897, Cap had more than proven himself on the baseball diamond. As a player, he had won four N.L. batting titles. As a manager, he had won five pennants. To this day, he is the winningest manager in Cubs' history.

Anson was elected to the Baseball Hall of Fame in 1939. Today, there is a simple plaque below his picture in those hallowed halls. It says "Greatest hitter and greatest National League player-manager of the 19th century."

THE SECONDARY DYNASTY

After Anson retired in 1897, the Cubs spent several years in the middle of the N.L. standings before giving Chicago its second baseball dynasty. By 1903, when the first World Series was held, Chicago had moved back up to third. The Cubs placed second in 1904 and third again in 1905.

The players who helped take Chicago back to the top were an interesting combination. The batting leader turned out to be Harry Steinfelt, a third baseman who could more than handle his own in the top "hot corner". King of the outfield was Wildfire Schulte. Catcher Johnny King got better each year.

And no one could forget the Cubs pitchers. There was Mordecai "Three-finger" Brown. Though he had lost part of the index finger and mangled his little finger on his pitching hand in a corn shredder when he was seven years old, Brown became Chicago's ace. He was backed up by Ed Reulbach, Jack Pfiester and Carl Lundgren — all powerful pitchers in their own right.

Adrian "Cap" Ason manager the Cubs to five pennants between 1880 and 1886. He was voted the greatest hitter and manager of the 19th Century.

POPULAR PLAYER, POPULAR SONG

After he retired, Cap Anson went into vaudeville and did a traveling entertainment show. At one of these shows, a songwriter by the name of Jack Norworth asked Anson if he would introduce a new song on his show. Anson agreed, and the song, "Take Me Out to the Ball Game" became another baseball tradition.

13

SHUTOUT KING
On September 26, 1908, in the midst of Chicago's memorable pennant race with the Giants, Cubs pitcher Ed Reulbach won both halves of a doubleheader in two shutouts. He blanked Brooklyn 5-0 on five hits, and 3-0 on three hits. He walked only one and threw only one wild pitch.

TINKERS-TO-EVERS-TO-CHANCE

The real stars of the Cubs' second dynasty were a legendary trio of infielders: Joe Tinker at short, Johnny Evers at second and Frank Chance at first. In baseball scorer's lingo, a Cubs' double play was called "Tinker to Evers to Chance," and that phrase became so popular that New York sportswriter Franklin P. Adams actually wrote a poem about it:

These are the saddest of possible words,
   Tinker-to-Evers-to-Chance.
Trio of Bear Cubs fleeter than birds,
   Tinker-to-Evers-to-Chance.
Pricking our gonfalon bubble,
Making a Giant hit into a double,
Words that are weighty with nothing but trouble,
   Tinker-to-Evers-to-Chance.

The strange part about the legend of Tinker to Evers to Chance is that the trio wasn't really a record-setting double-play combination. During four years at the height of their popularity, the three made only 56 double plays. A good major league team today might triple that number in *one* season. One year, Tinker hit only .233 and Evers led the league's second basemen with 44 errors.

But in the tradition of the Cubs, Tinker, Evers and Chance took the talent they had and made the best of it. In 1905, Chicago manager Frank Selee moved Tinker from third base to shortstop, Chance from catcher to first base and Evers from shortstop to second.

Many players today would walk off the field rather than undergo such drastic changes. But not these three. They learned their new positions the best they could, and the Chicago fans loved them for it. Joe Tinker was no slugger at the plate, although in 1908 he led the Cubs

Where's Chance? Joe Tinker (left) and Johnny Evers (right) needed Frank Chance at first to complete their legendary double plays.

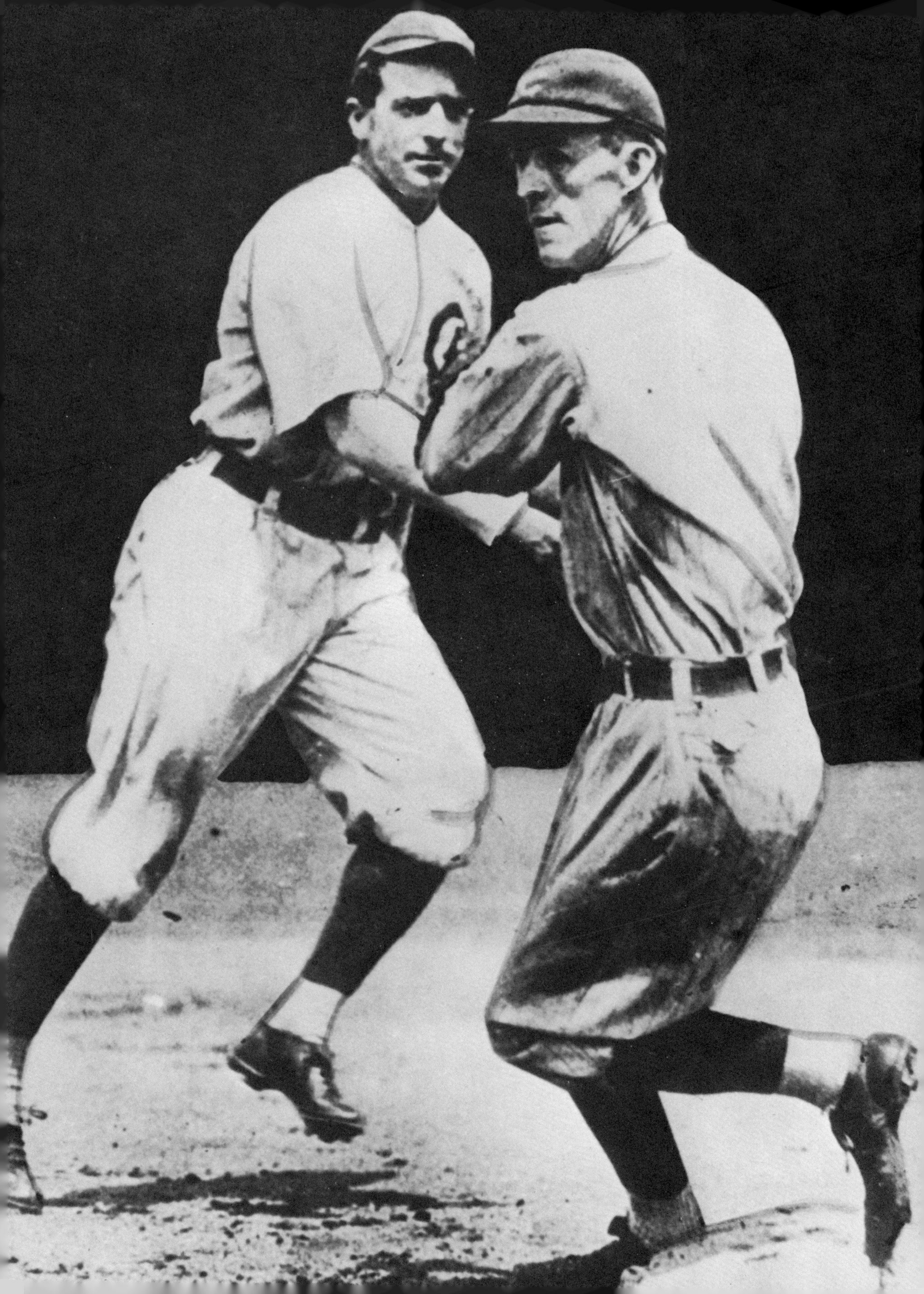

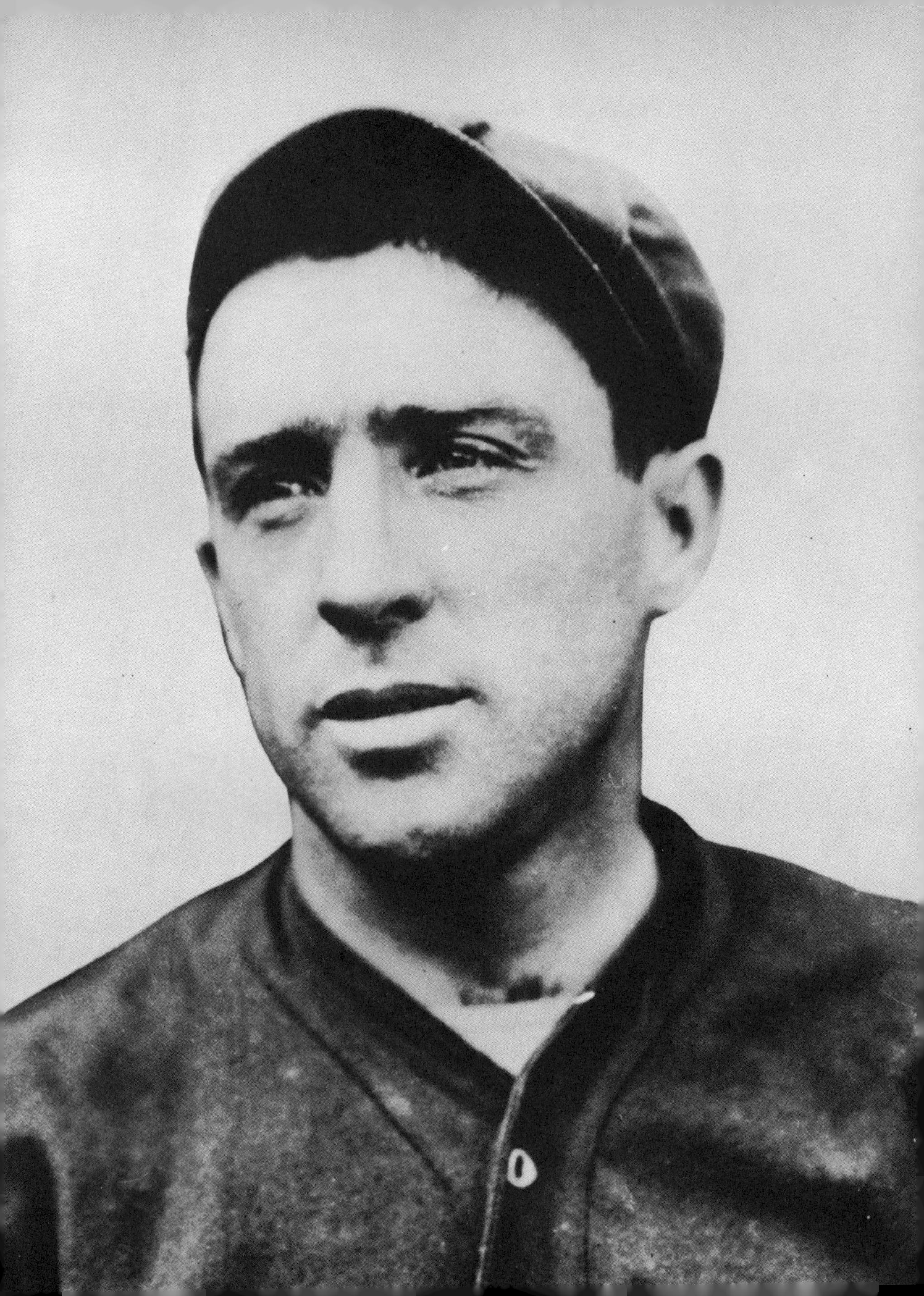

with seven home runs (the team combined for just 20). Tinker made up for any batting problems by becoming one of the finest fielding shortstops in baseball. He also had the sweetest disposition of the three.

Johnny Evers was so small and scrawny that he had to beg for his first minor-league tryout. But "The Crab," as he was finally nicknamed, was a guy who just wouldn't give up. As his experience deepened, Evers worked miracles on the baseball diamond.

Frank Chance was the team's leader. His teammates called him "Husk," because of his powerful, 200-pound build, and sportswriters tabbed him "The Peerless Leader." He had a quick mind and a powerful personality. Midway through the 1905 season, Chance was named manager by a vote of his players. It was under Chance that the Cubs won four National League pennants — and two World Series — in five years!

CHICAGO AGAINST CHICAGO

The streak began in 1906, when the Cubs won 116 of 152 games, a .763 winning percentage. That's still the best mark in modern major-league history. Chicago breezed to the 1906 N.L. pennant, winning by 20 games.

Steinfeldt batted .327 and led the league in runs batted in with 83. He also had the leading fielding percentage for National League third basemen. Chance batted .317 and Kling .312. Six of eight Cubs pitchers won ten or more games. The Cubs also led all N.L. teams in overall batting average, with .282.

Still, the Cubs didn't get as much attention as they deserved during the season. While the Cubs were winning their pennant by a comfortable margin, many Chicago baseball fans were going across town to watch the rival American League White Sox, who were locked in a much closer pennant race. The Sox won 19 straight con-

In 1905, Joe Tinker was moved from third base to shortstop, where he became one of the sweetest fielders in baseball history.

BAD LUCK
On May 2, 1917, Chicago pitcher Jim "Hippo" Vaughn did what most pitchers can only dream of doing: He pitched 9-1/3 innings of no-hit ball. But Vaughn lost the game to Cincinnati, 1-0, after giving up only two hits to the Reds.

CRAZY RECORD
The Philadelphia Phillies sometimes are called "The Fightin' Phillies." That nickname may have come in a game against the Cubs on August 5, 1922. The Cubs held a 25-6 lead when Philadelphia staged a magnificent rally. When the dust cleared, the two teams had combined for 49 runs and 51 hits in 9 innings — one of baseball's craziest records.

tests in August and captured the flag by a mere three games. That set up the first all-Chicago World Series.

Baseball experts said the White Sox didn't have a chance against the Cubs. The White Sox had earned the nickname "Hitless Wonders" during the season because as a team they had batted only .228, lowest in the major leagues.

The strength of the White Sox was in their pitching. Much to the Cubs' dismay, the Series turned into a duel on the mound. Unheralded Nick Altrock beat Brown in Game 1 to give the Sox the lift they needed. Then in Games 5 and 6, the Hitless Wonders found their groove and beat the Cubs 8-6 and 8-3 to win the Series, 4 games to 2.

REVENGE

The Cubs got their revenge the next season. They won the pennant by 17 games and were ready when legendary Ty Cobb and the Detroit Tigers took the A.L. flag. Chicago's pitchers earned four wins and one tie in five games to earn their first world championship.

The 1908 pennant race actually overshadowed Chicago's second straight World Series title. Three teams — Chicago, Pittsburgh and the New York Giants — were in the race for the flag almost from Opening Day in April. The Cubs had the early lead. But the Pirates, led by colorful shortstop Honus Wagner, took the lead in July. By August, the Giants and pitcher Christy Mathewson were in first.

Strangely, the Cubs may have actually won the Pennant by losing a game on September 4. Here's what happened:

Chicago was deadlocked with Pittsburgh 0-0 in the last of the ninth inning when the Pirates put runners on first and third. The next Pittsburgh batter singled to drive in

Mordecai Brown (left) talks with catcher Jimmy Archer before an Old Timers Game at the 1933 Chicago World's Fair. In 1908, they were the scourge of the National League.

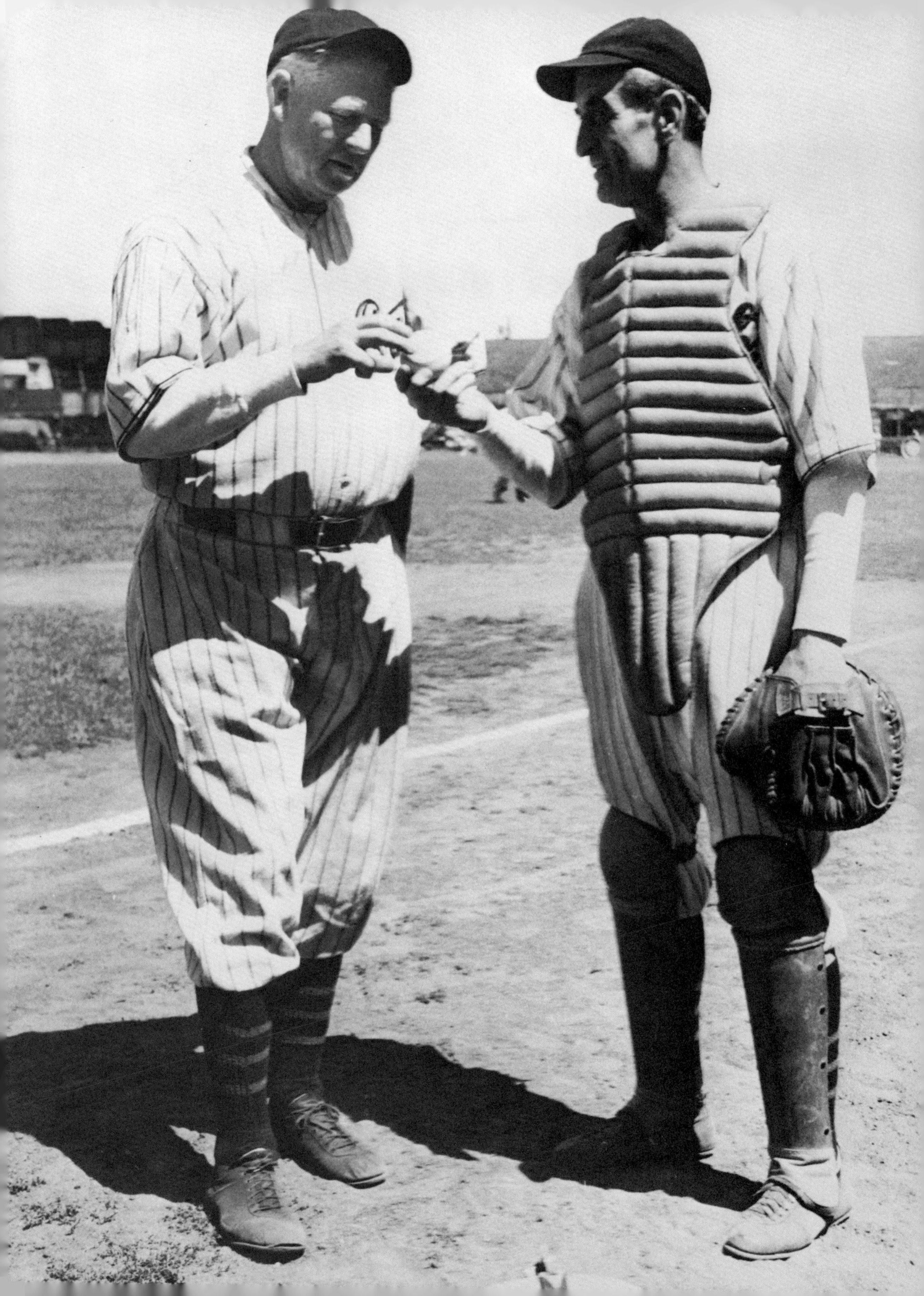

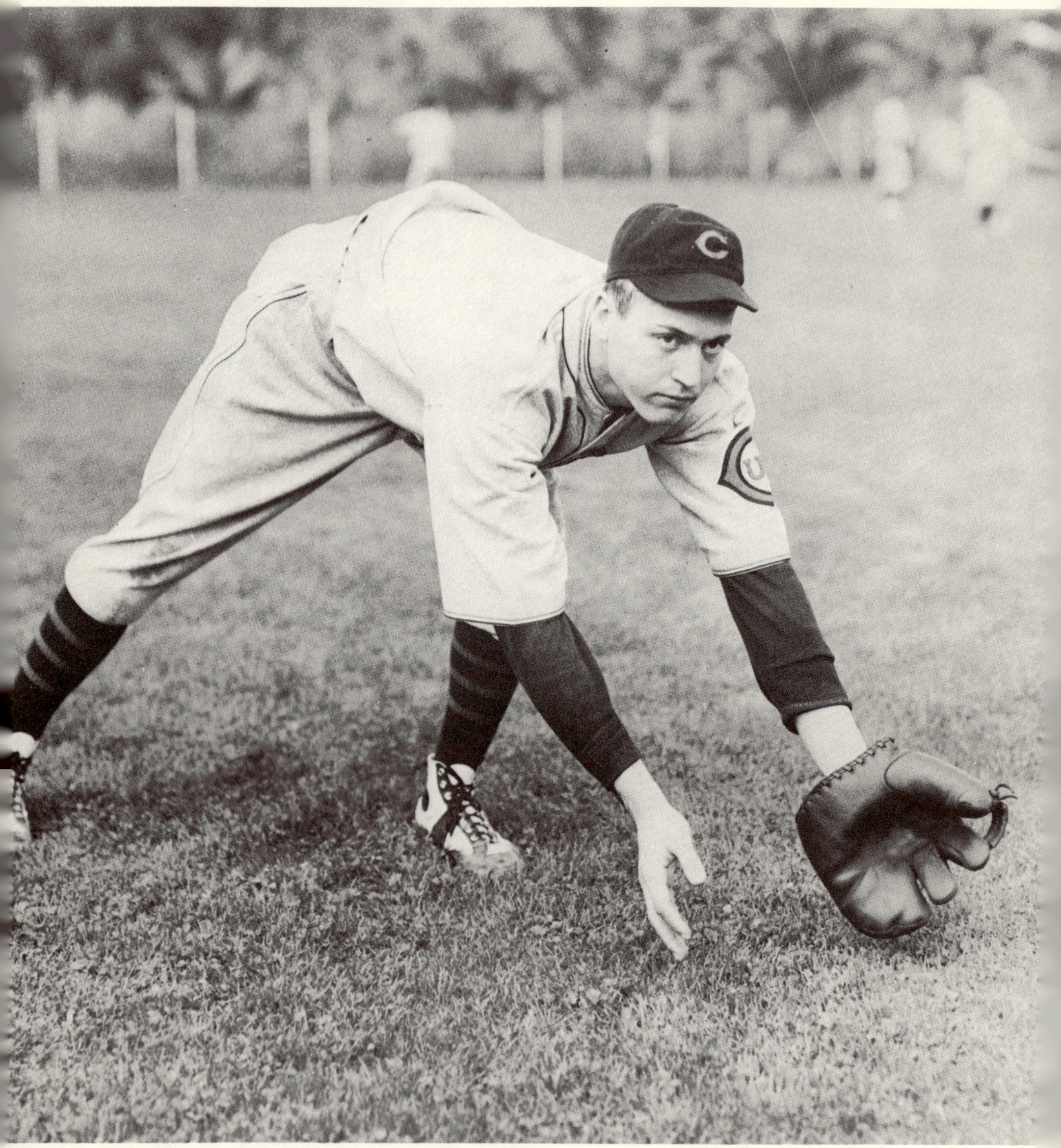

the winning run. Like many base runners of that time, the Pirate runner at first didn't bother with the formality of touching second base. As soon as he saw his teammate touch home, he headed for the dugout himself.

Johnny Evers saw what the Pirate runner had done. He got the ball and tagged second. He told umpire Hank O'Day that the runner at first had been forced out and that the run should not count. But O'Day didn't listen, and the Pirates won the game.

Evers told manager Frank Chance about the incident. Chance quietly complained to N.L. officials, and soon even O'Day realized he had been wrong. He vowed to enforce the rule ("No run can score when the final out of an inning is a force play") the next time the play occurred.

It happened sooner than he might have imagined. In a crucial series against the Giants, Brown saved the first half of a doubleheader and won the second to get the Cubs rolling. The next day, one of baseball's most memorable events occurred.

The score again was tied, 1-1, in the bottom of the ninth. The Giants came to bat. With one out, Moose McCormick singled. Fred Merkel, a 19-year-old rookie playing his first full major-league game at first base, surprised everyone by also singling, sending McCormick to third. Al Bridwell smacked a line drive to center, and the Giants appeared to have won the game when McCormick trotted across home plate and fans raced onto the field to mob the Giants.

But crafty Johnny Evers noticed that in the confusion, Merkle had forgotten to touch second and had run instead toward the clubhouse in deep center field. The ball also got lost in the confusion, but Evers finally retrieved it and stepped on second, making sure the umpire saw him.

William Herman, the Cubs' baby-faced infielder, plugs the gap at 1932 Spring Training.

UNPOPULAR TRADE
Cubs' fans were outraged in 1941 when the team traded popular second baseman Billy Herman to the Brooklyn Dodgers. Herman's smooth, level swing had earned him a .314 average during Chicago's 1932 pennant drive. Charlie Grimm later would say that on today's market, Herman would be worth at least one million dollars.

THE MANAGER THAT GOT AWAY

After Joe McCarthy left the Cubs and joined the New York Yankees, his success increased. By the time he retired in 1950, McCarthy had won 2,126 games and lost just 1,335, for a winning percentage of .614. He still is major-league baseball's winningest manager ever.

The umpire was Hank O'Day. "He's out. The run doesn't count," O'Day said. He called the game a 1-1 tie, because of the confusion on the field. The game was replayed after the two teams finished the regular season tied with identical 98-55 records.

There were plenty of hard feelings between the teams for that final game. Several Cub players were threatened with physical harm if they played and beat the Giants. They still played, of course — in front of more than 35,000 fans, the largest crowd ever to see a game up to that time.

The great Christy Mathewson had already won 35 games for the Giants that season. New York fans wanted just one more. But it was not to be. Three-Finger Brown came in for Jack Pfiester in the first inning and held the Giants to two runs. Johnny Kling, Frank Schulte and Frank Chance drove in four runs to give Chicago a 4-2 win and the pennant.

A near-riot by angry giant fans left Pfiester with a knife slash, but the Cubs had won the flag again. That was what counted.

After a tough battle like that one, it wouldn't have been surprising if the Cubs let down against the Tigers in the World Series. They didn't, of course. Chance batted .421 and stole five bases. Brown and Orval Overall each won two games as the Tigers were caged in five games. The Cubs were kings again!

The letdown finally did arrive, however, in 1909. Though the Cubs still won 104 games, they couldn't beat the Pirates for the pennant.

The last National League championship for the Cubs' 20th-century dynasty came in 1910. This time, 104 wins was good enough for the pennant. But the Chicago team closed out its dynasty as it had been started, with an upset loss.

He was small and scrawny, but Johnny Evers could work miracles in the infield.

23

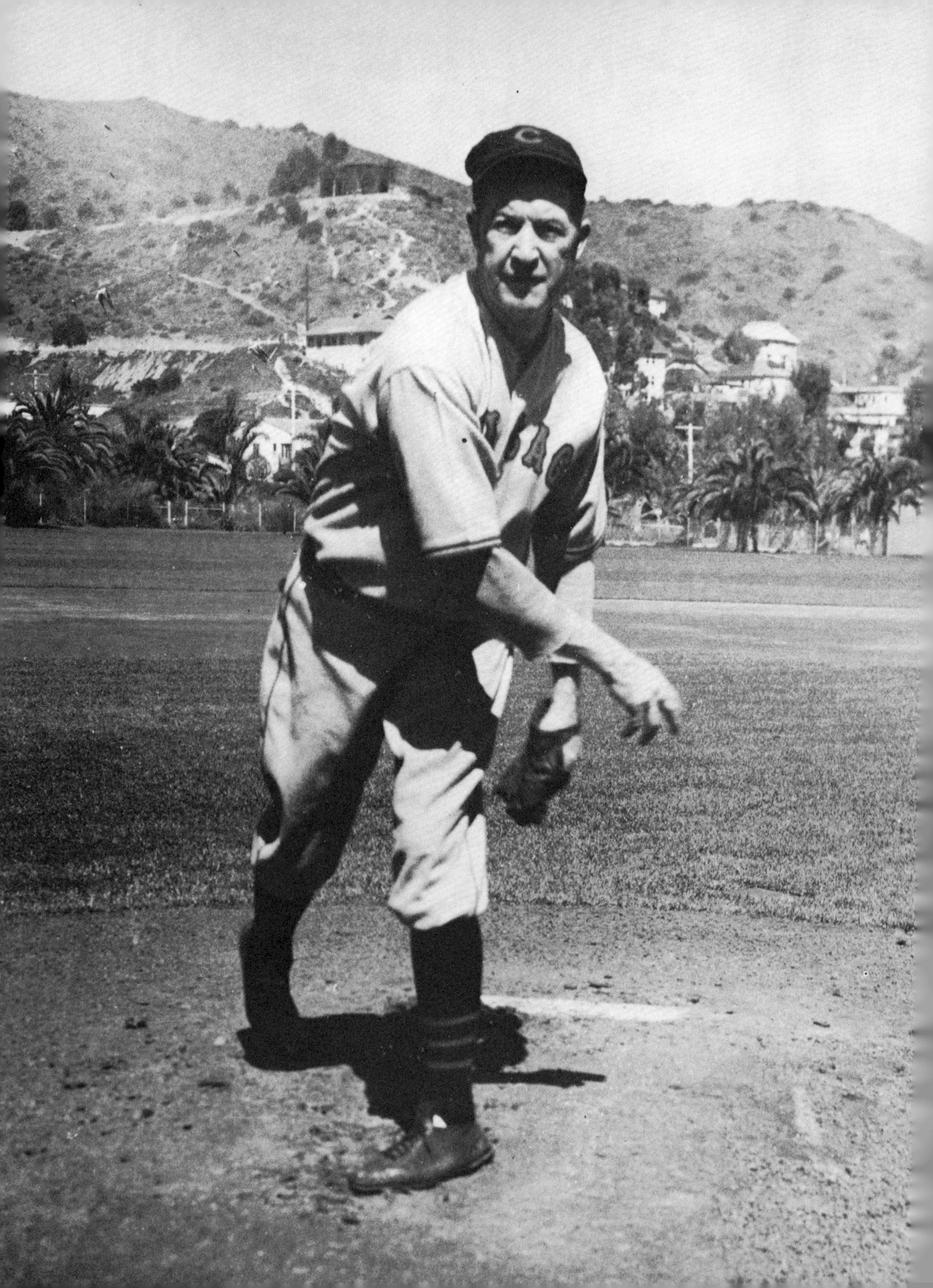

The spoilers in 1910 were a bunch of kids under the cunning care of Philadelphia manager Connie Mack. Mack had toured college campuses and picked out the smartest and quickest players he saw. It took him only three years to build a powerful baseball machine, and the Cubs were one of its victims.

The famous Chicago pitchers were squeezed by the A's for a .316 team batting average, a record that stood until 1960. Philly beat the Cubs, 4 games to 1.

THE DYNASTY WINDS DOWN

For any dynasty to continue, a team must have strong young players waiting in the wings to take over when the veterans retire.

That was not the case in Chicago. The Cubs finished second in 1911, third in 1912 and 1913, and kept dropping. Except for one glorious season, they didn't place higher than third again until 1929.

But that one year, 1918, was enough to keep the hopes of Cubs' fans alive. Under manager Fred Mitchell, Chicago won 84 games, lost 45 and won their fifth N.L. pennant of the modern era.

Much of the Cubs' strength again came from its pitching. This time, though, the leader on the mound was the one-and-only Grover Cleveland Alexander. He had come to Chicago along with catcher Bill Killefer from Philadelphia for $60,000 and two Cubs.

When World Series time came around, the Cubs were the weaker club. How could that be? Well, Grover Alexander had enlisted in the armed forces because of World War I. And Boston, the A.L. representative, had a bright new prospect who could defeat a team single-handed. His name was Babe Ruth. The Red Sox won the Series, 4 games to 2.

After his retirement, the great Grover Cleveland Alexander came to training camp to pitch batting practice for the Cubs.

YOU CAN CALL ME... Stan Hack, the Cubs' third baseman from 1932 to 1947, was nicknamed "Flake." Once, during a rain delay, the fun-loving infielder climbed a 75-foot light tower and nearly scared his manager to death. In 16 years, Hack hit .301.

LOTS OF FANS
More than one million people live within one mile of the Cubs' ballpark. Even though Wrigley Field holds only 36,645 people, low by major-league standards, the team has drawn more than one million fans every year since 1968, and 12 seasons before then.

Other exciting things were happening to the Cubs, though, even when they weren't adding pennants to their collection. First on the list was a change of ownership in 1915.

William Wrigley Jr. was the owner of the huge chewing gum company that made Juicy Fruit and several other favorite American flavors. He already owned one semi-pro baseball team in 1915, which was known as the Juicy Fruit or the Wrigleys.

But one day that year, Wrigley was taking a trip by train when he got into an interesting conversation with a fellow passenger.

"How come a Cincinnati family owns a baseball team in Chicago?", the passenger asked. "I would think that Chicago's lack of interest in the Cubs could give the city a black eye."

Wrigley sat back and thought about that. "What you say is both interesting and true," he replied. "I will look into the situation at my first opportunity."

WRIGLEY POWER!

That opportunity came on January 20, 1916. Wrigley joined a partnership that bought the Cubs from the Taft family of Cincinnati. Wrigley became director of that partnership. In 1921 he became majority stockholder.

Thus began the powerful influence of the Wrigley family on the Cubs, the National League and major-league baseball.

In 1919, when the cross-town White Sox scandalized the league with reports of cheating and "throwing" World Series games, Wrigley led the push to appoint Judge Keenesaw Mountain Landis as commissioner of baseball.

Some didn't want Landis to have absolute power over the sport, but Wrigley wouldn't back down. Landis got

Bill Wrigley, Jr., the "chewing gum giant," bought the Cubs and fought for them. His son, Phil Wrigley, took over from 1932 to 1977.

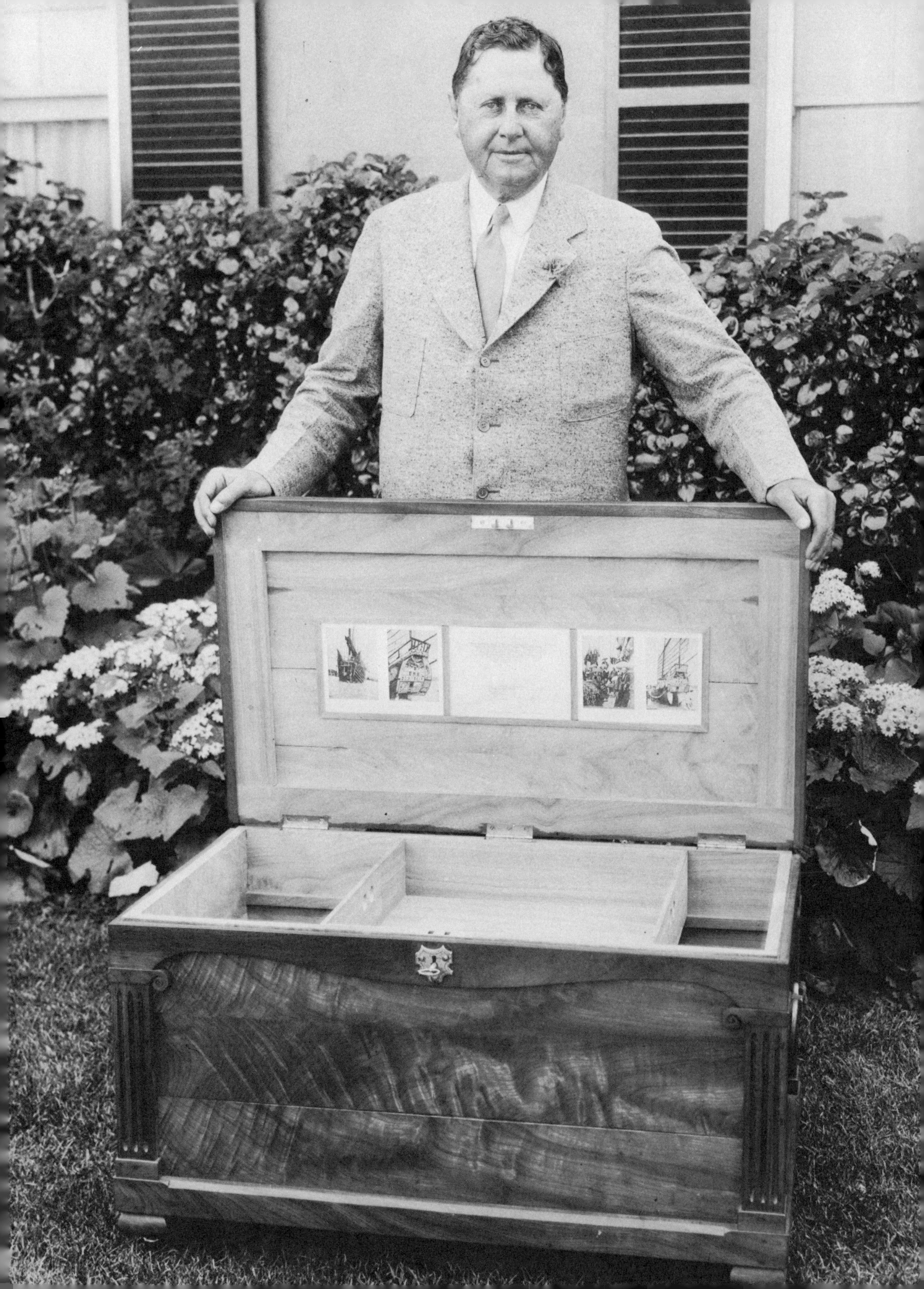

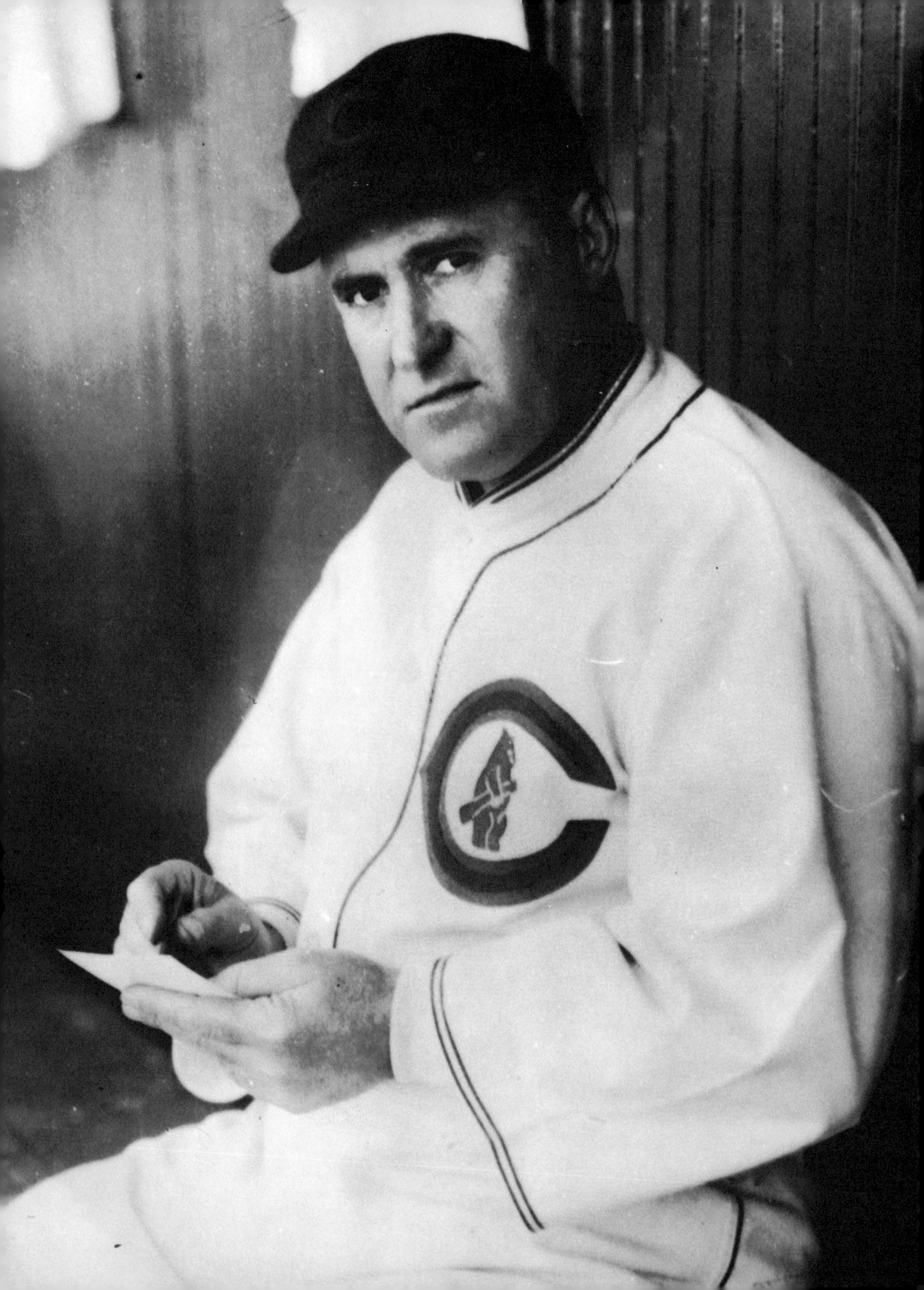

the job (and the power), and baseball became better because of it.

William Wrigley Jr. died in 1932. Sadly, he had never experienced the joy of seeing a World championship. His son, Philip K. Wrigley, took over.

Phil Wrigley ran the club until his death in 1977. In those 45 years, he did many positive things to the Cubs' relationship with their fans, the city and the league:

• He helped form baseball's association with radio and television, and helped spread the goodwill of the Cubs to fans across the country.

• He helped pass some of baseball's most important rules changes and helped create the N.L.'s two-division format.

• He started a policy of always keeping the interest of the fans and the sport above his own club. "We're only as strong as the league," Wrigley would say. He could have vetoed the Boston Braves' move to Milwaukee, since Milwaukee was close enough to Chicago to disturb the Cubs' attendance. But he let the Braves move, because he knew the franchise wouldn't survive in Boston.

Phil Wrigley didn't go to many of Chicago's games. But he probably was closer to his team than any other owner. The Cubs admired and respected him for caring about them as people, not just ballplayers. And they responded by giving Wrigley — and Chicago — their very best.

THE ROAD BACK TO THE TOP

The Cubs fought their way back to the top of the National League by 1929, and stayed there, off and on, through 1945. During those 17 seasons, Chicago won five more pennants. But they still couldn't win another World Series.

An all-star cast began to arrive in 1922, when Charles Leo Hartnett came on the Chicago scene. The 6-1,

In 1930, Joe McCarthy was manager of the Cubs. In 1932, he was manager of the Yankees when the Yanks defeated the Cubs in the World Series.

SMALL WORLD
Joe McCarthy and Bill Wrigley grew up in the same neighborhood of Germantown, Pennsylvania. They discovered that fact when the two met, for the first time, when Wrigley hired McCarthy to manage the Cubs.

WHY NO LIGHTS? Let Phil Wrigley explain why he never installed lights at Wrigley Field: "I've always felt the game should be played in the daylight," Wrigley once said. "Besides, we don't want to disturb our neighbors."

215-pound catcher was one of the finest defensive players in baseball history. Hartnett's arm was so strong that fans would come to the game early just to watch him whip the ball from base to base.

Behind the plate, Hartnett talked so much that the sportswriters called him "Gabby." In the batting department, Leo (he didn't like to be called Charles) had a career average of .297. He stayed with the Cubs until 1940.

Two more stars — and a new manager — put on Cubs uniforms in 1926. Off the field, Riggs Stephenson was a gentle southern gentleman from Alabama. At the plate, however, Stephenson went after pitches like a wounded lion. He batted .362 with 110 RBI in 1929, and .324 with 85 RBI in 1932. Hack Wilson also joined the Cubs in 1926. He was a stubby, strong batter who made his biggest contributions in 1929. In '29, he hit .400 in the World Series. But a play in which he lost a ball in the sun and allowed a Philadelphia rally to continue, earned him the name "Sonny Boy."

Wilson didn't like the nickname. He showed his displeasure in 1930, when he hit a N.L. record 56 home runs, batted in 190 runs, sliced 35 doubles and recorded a .723 slugging percentage. The old nickname was buried, replaced by "Li'l Round Man."

The new manager in 1926 was Joe McCarthy. McCarthy had been a minor-league manager in Louisville before Wrigley and team president Bill Veeck offered him the reins to the Cubs. They then helped out the young skipper by adding several more good players, including pitchers Charley Root and Pat Malone, Hazen "Kiki" Cuyler, and a sure-handed second baseman named Rogers Hornsby.

Hornsby and Detroit's Ty Cobb were two of baseball's most disliked players. Hornsby's problem was that he

Gabby Hartnett is credited with hitting "the most exciting home run in Cubs history" — a pennant-winning boomer at dusk.

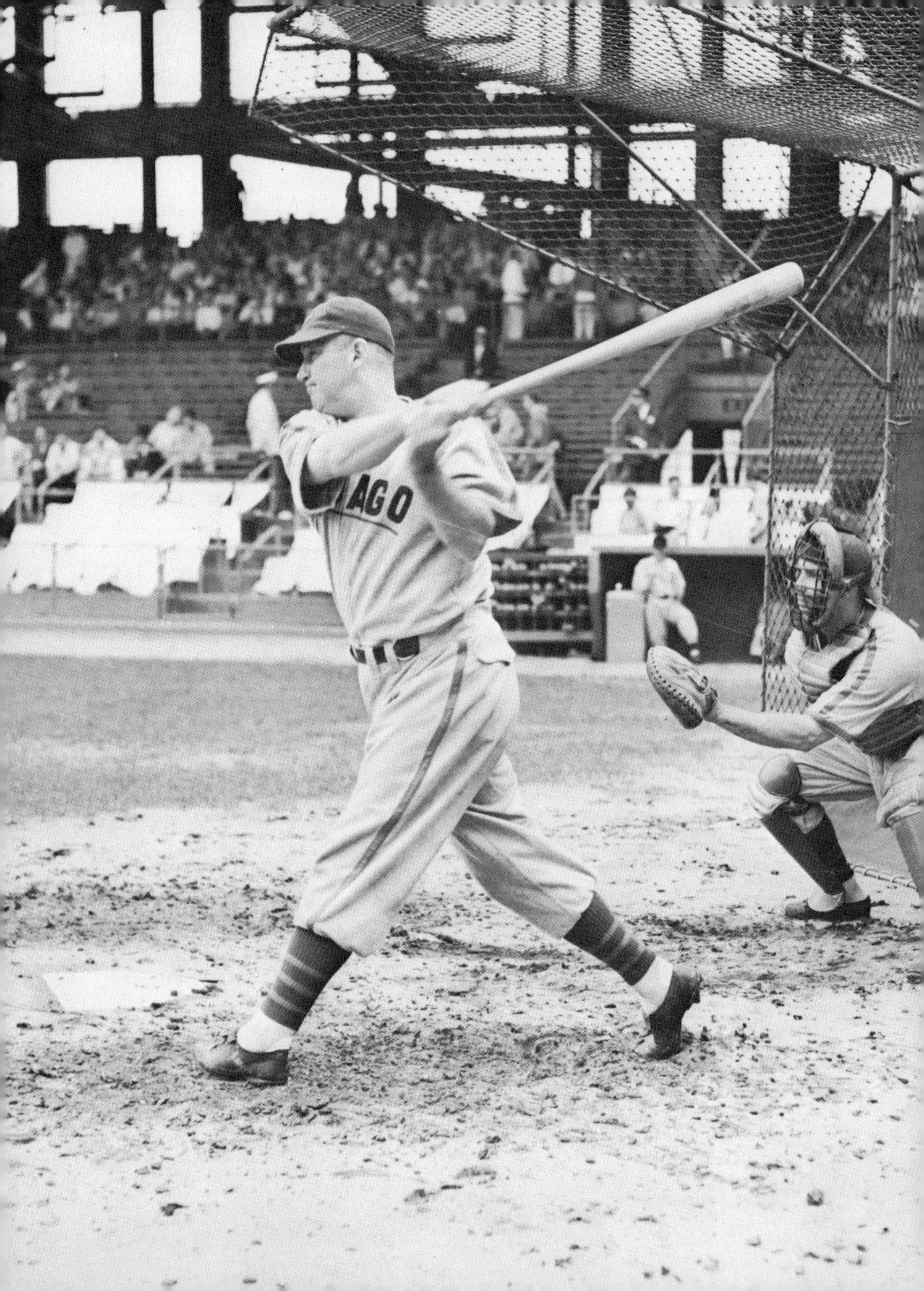

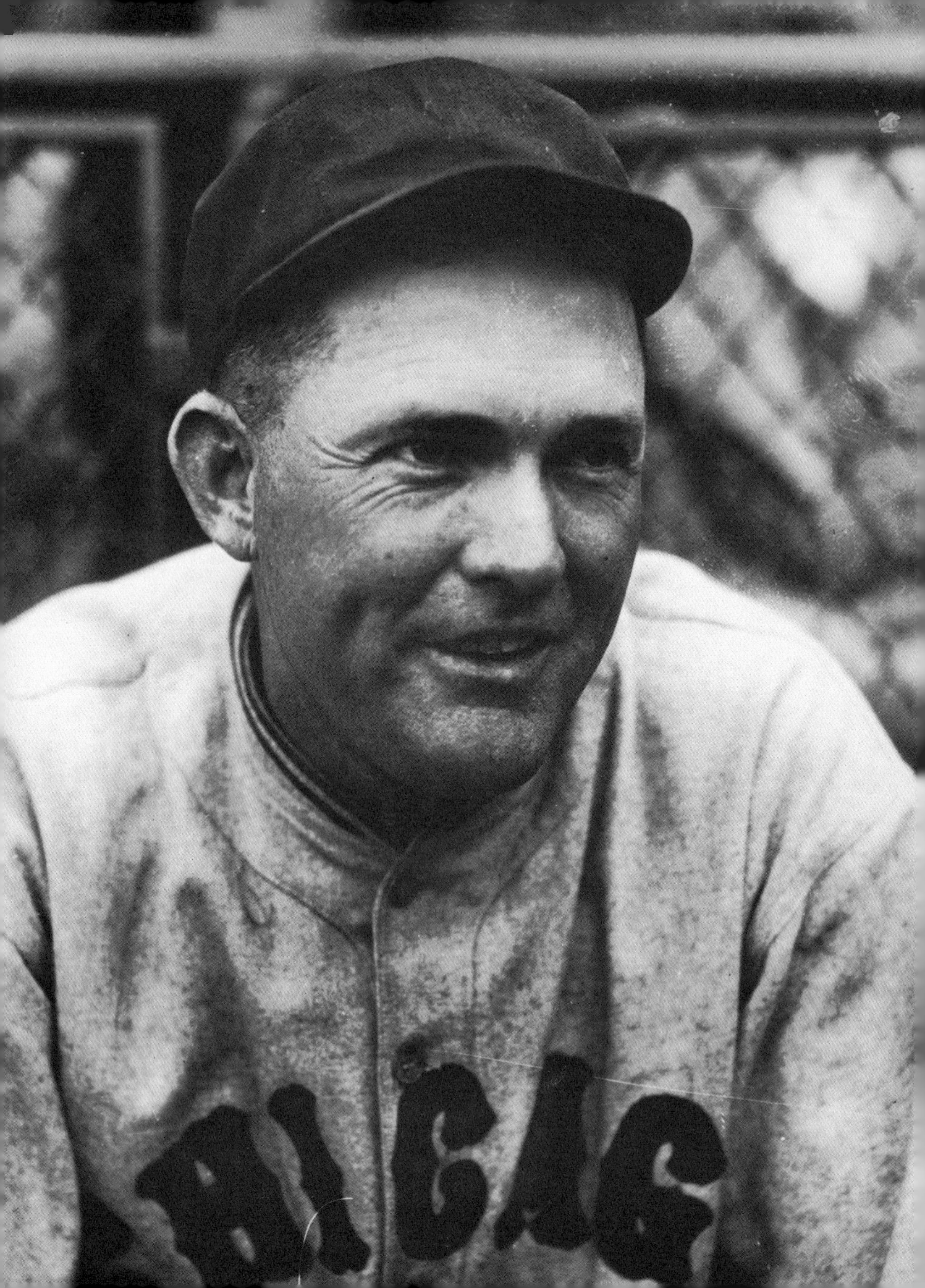

could be too blunt — he would criticize others to their faces, with no regard for their feelings. At the plate, of course, Hornsby was one of the best boomers ever. His lifetime batting average of .358 is second only to Cobb.

It was this crew that led the Cubs to the 1929 National League pennant with a 98-54 record. Hornsby hit .380, Stephenson .362, Cuyler .360 and Wilson .345 with 39 homers.

But crafty old Connie Mack and his Philadelphia A's were back in the Series again, too.

Mack surprised even his own team when he started 35-year-old Howard Ehmke in Game 1 of the championship. The strategy worked. The Cubs couldn't get their bats on Ehmke's molasses-slow pitches. The A's took Game 2 as well, but Chicago rebounded to win the third game.

Game 4 was the Cubs' real downfall. It preceded by just a few days the famous stock market crash of 1929, but in the Windy City the effects were almost as devastating.

Chicago took an 8-0 lead into the seventh inning, and still lost the game. When they lost the next game, too, they dropped their chance for a Series title.

Hornsby took over as manager mid-way through the next season, when McCarthy was lured to the New York Yankees. Hornsby and Charlie Grimm split managing duties in 1932, when another flag came Chicago's way.

Unfortunately for the Cubs, their World Series opponent was New York, managed by — you guessed it — Joe McCarthy. In only four games, the Yankees blasted 45 hits to destroy the Cubs. Lou Gehrig averaged .529 at the plate, with three homers and eight runs batted in.

But that Series is best known for a play between Cubs

In 1929, the immortal Rogers Hornsby already had seven National League batting titles to his credit. That year he did it again with a .380 average.

WELCOME TO CHICAGO
Rogers Hornsby came to Chicago with a big reputation. In his second game with the Cubs, when he struck out with the bases loaded, the Chicago fans let him know that they expected better. The fiery Hornsby won back their hearts on his very next at-bat. Again the bases were loaded, but this time "The Rajah" drove the ball out of the ballpark.

COLLEGE OF COACHES
For five years, 1961-1965, the Cubs actually played with no manager at all. Instead, the team was run by a group of specialized coaches. Phil Wrigley began the unique approach to coaching because he felt the Cubs were not schooled in the basics of baseball. The different coaches took turns managing the team.

pitcher Charley Root and New York's immortal slugger, Babe Ruth.

Ruth had hit a three-run round-tripper earlier in the game, so the Babe already had a bit of a good-natured yelling match going with the Chicago fans when he came to the plate in the fifth inning.

The Cubs' bench and fans heckled Ruth as he watched a strike zing past him. Babe stepped out of the batter's box and held up one finger.

Another strike hit the catcher's mitt. Ruth held up two fingers, and then waved his hand in the direction of the centerfield bleachers.

Some people say the Babe simply was indicating that he had one more strike remaining. But others think the Bambino was pointing to the centerfield stands, where he intended to put the next pitch.

Root wound up and let loose with pitch number three. Ruth swung. At that instant, there was no doubt where that ball was headed. it landed squarely in the centerfield bleachers. Ruth trotted around the bases as the Cubs dugout sat stunned and the Chicago fans howled in disbelief. Another Babe Ruth yarn had been spun.

THE '35 PENNANT

The Cubs' pennant win in 1935 took a great come-from-behind effort. Chicago won 21 late-season games in a row — and 100 overall — to sweep past the defending N.L. champs, the St. Louis Cardinals.

Still, the World Series championship remained out of Chicago's reach. This time, the Detroit Tigers dashed the Cubs' hopes in six games.

The back-breaker came in Game 6. The score was tied 3-3 when Chicago's Stan Hack led off the ninth with a triple. That's where he stayed for the next three outs, as his teammates tried without success to send him

Hazen "Kiki" Cuyler, the clouting Chicago outfielder, helped lead the Cubs to the 1929 pennant with a .360 batting average.

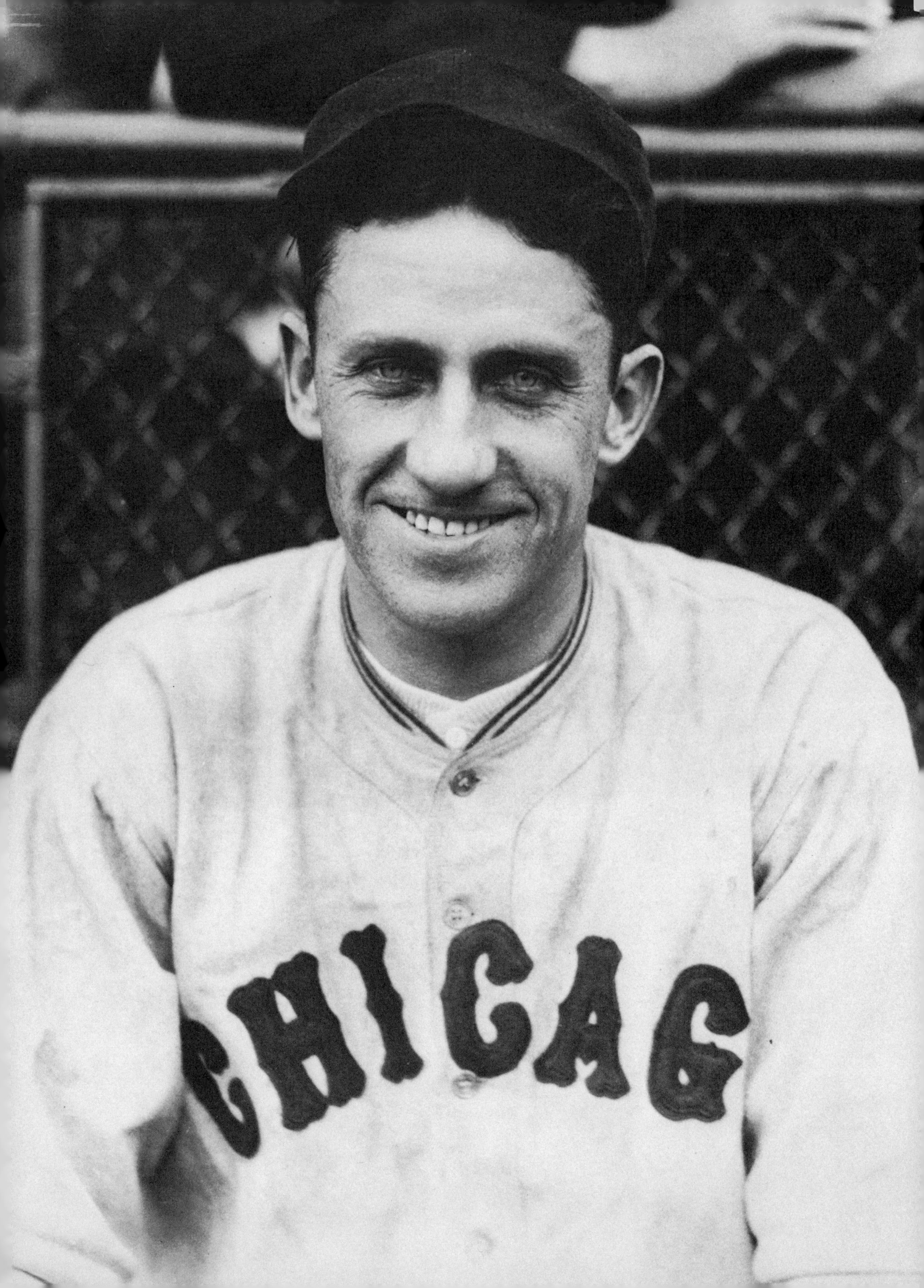
CHICAG

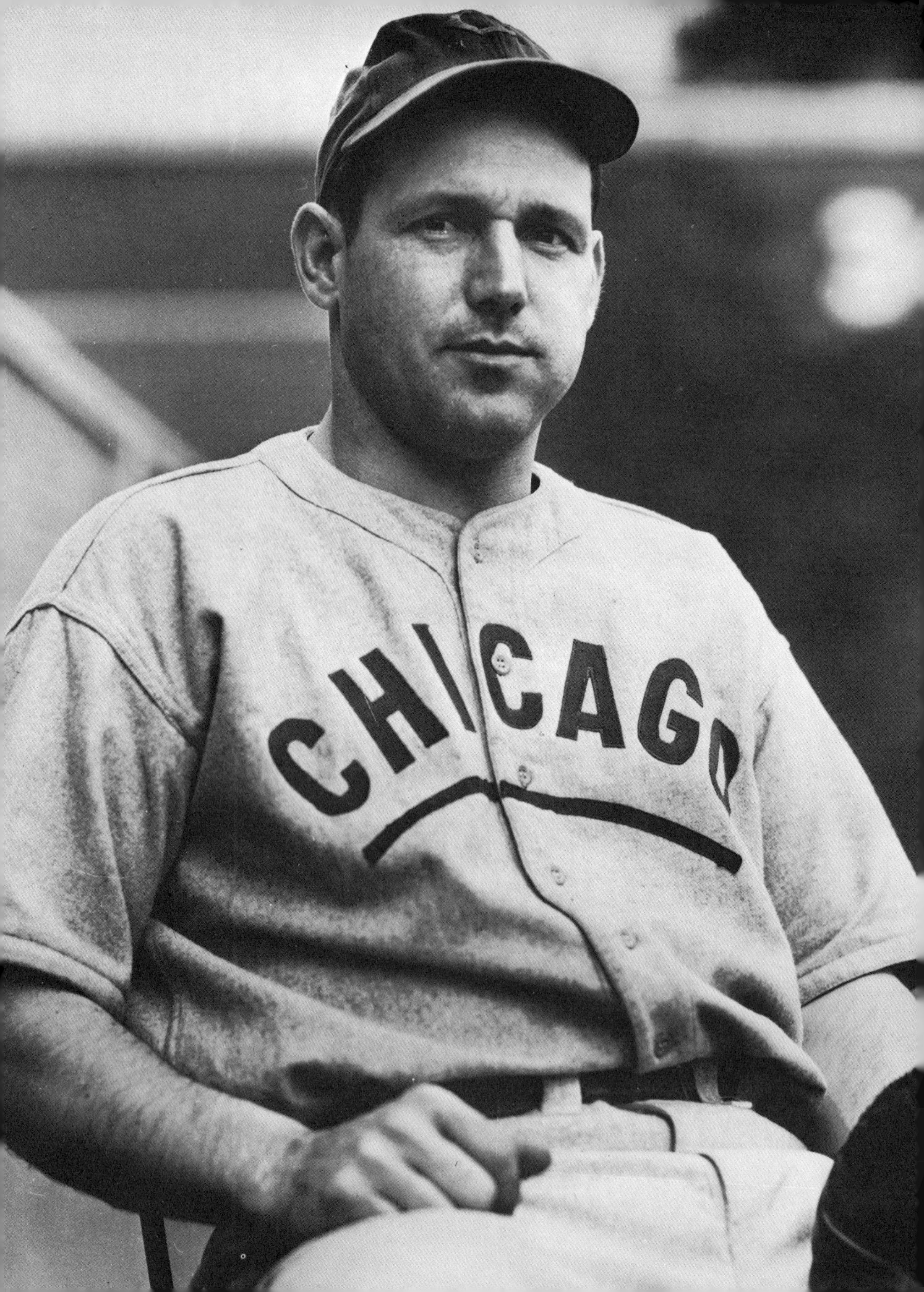
CHICAGO

home. The Tigers scored in their half, and the title was theirs.

Chicago's next World Series appearance was almost overshadowed by something that had happened when the Cubs were earning the pennant.

This time, the Pittsburgh Pirates were challenging the Cubs for the National League pennant. The Pirates held a half-game lead over the Cubs.

The score was tied as Chicago came to bat in the bottom of the ninth. The sun had set and darkness was closing in on Wrigley field which does not have artificial lights.

Gabby Hartnett stepped into the batter's box. He was player-manager of the Cubs then, and he had to face Mace Brown, Pittsburgh's tough relief pitcher.

Two outs, no one on base. The fans squinted into the fading light. Brown released his pitch. Gabby swung at where he "thought" the ball would be — it was that dark. He met the ball squarely and rocketed it back into the left-field bleacher seats. The Cubs won the game and the pennant with the most exciting home run in Chicago history.

Years later, even Phil Wrigley would admit that Gabby's homer was his most memorable Cubs moment.

McCarthy's Yankees were Chicago's World Series demons again, and again in only four games. Despite a courageous performance by an injured Dizzy Dean, the All-Star pitcher who had been obtained by the Cubs from St. Louis midway through the season, the Yanks took it all.

NEVER STOP CHEERING

Chicago's last great hurrah — as far as pennants go — came in 1945. Most of the major-league teams had skeleton lineups because the strongest young men had been

Outfielder William Nicholson looked glum as the Cubs headed into the season of '47. It would be two decades before the mighty Cubs would once again become a power.

SO CLOSE
No Chicago Cubs pitcher has ever thrown a perfect game (allowing no batters to reach base). Milt Pappas came the closest on Sept. 2, 1972, when he walked a San Diego Padres player with two outs in the ninth inning.

JOLLY CHOLLY Charlie Grimm who managed the Cubs three different times (1932-38; 1944-49; and 1960), was a little superstitious. During the first win of Chicago's 21-game victory streak late in the 1935 season, he discovered a tack in his shoe. For the next 20 games, he faithfully drove a new tack into his shoe, to keep the streak going.

called to service for World War II.

Still, the Cubs did their best. Charlie Grimm again was managing, which was probably a good idea because Chicago had one of the funnest, happy-go-lucky teams ever. Grimm's good humor helped keep the Cubs loose.

Chicago battled the Giants and the Dodgers all season long, but they wound up on top with league-leading team batting (.277) and fielding (.980) averages.

Phil Cavaretta led the league with a .355 batting average; Stan Hack was the best third baseman in the league; and Andy Pafko led the team with 110 runs batted in.

Those familiar Detroit Tigers were hot, as they headed into the World Series. They had won the American League pennant on the last day of the season, behind Hammerin' Hank Greenberg's grand slam home run.

Pitcher Hank Borowy led the Cubs to a good start with a 9-0 thrashing of the Tigers in Game 1. Detroit came back to win Game 2, but Chicago took a 2-1 lead in the series when Claude Passeau tossed the World Series' second one-hitter ever for a 3-0 win.

The Tigers won games 4 and 5. Passeau got his second win in Game 6. In the seventh and deciding game, Detroit scored all the runs they needed (5) in the first inning, and went on to a 9-3 victory.

That, so far, has been the last of the Cubs' National League pennants and World Series appearances. But the Wrigley Field fans have never stopped cheering.

STARS WITH NO RINGS

Since that 1945 pennant, Cubs fans have seen hundreds of players come and go. Frequently their teams have been listed near the bottom of the National League standings.

But there have been other years in which the Cubs have come tantalizingly close to owning another N.L. flag.

The first workout. At 1933 spring training, Cubs' president Bill Veeck (left) and manager Charley Grimm survey the advance guard.

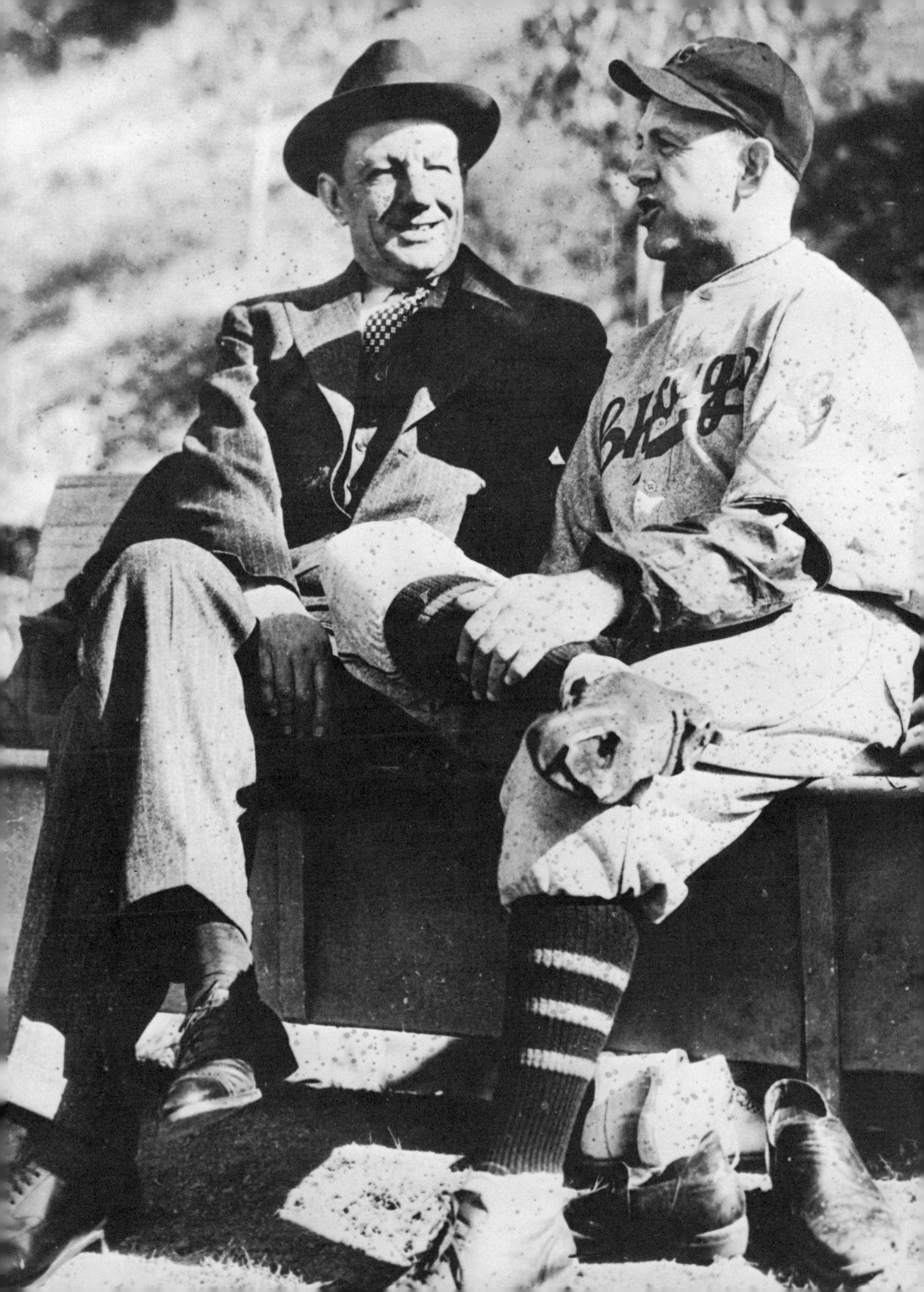

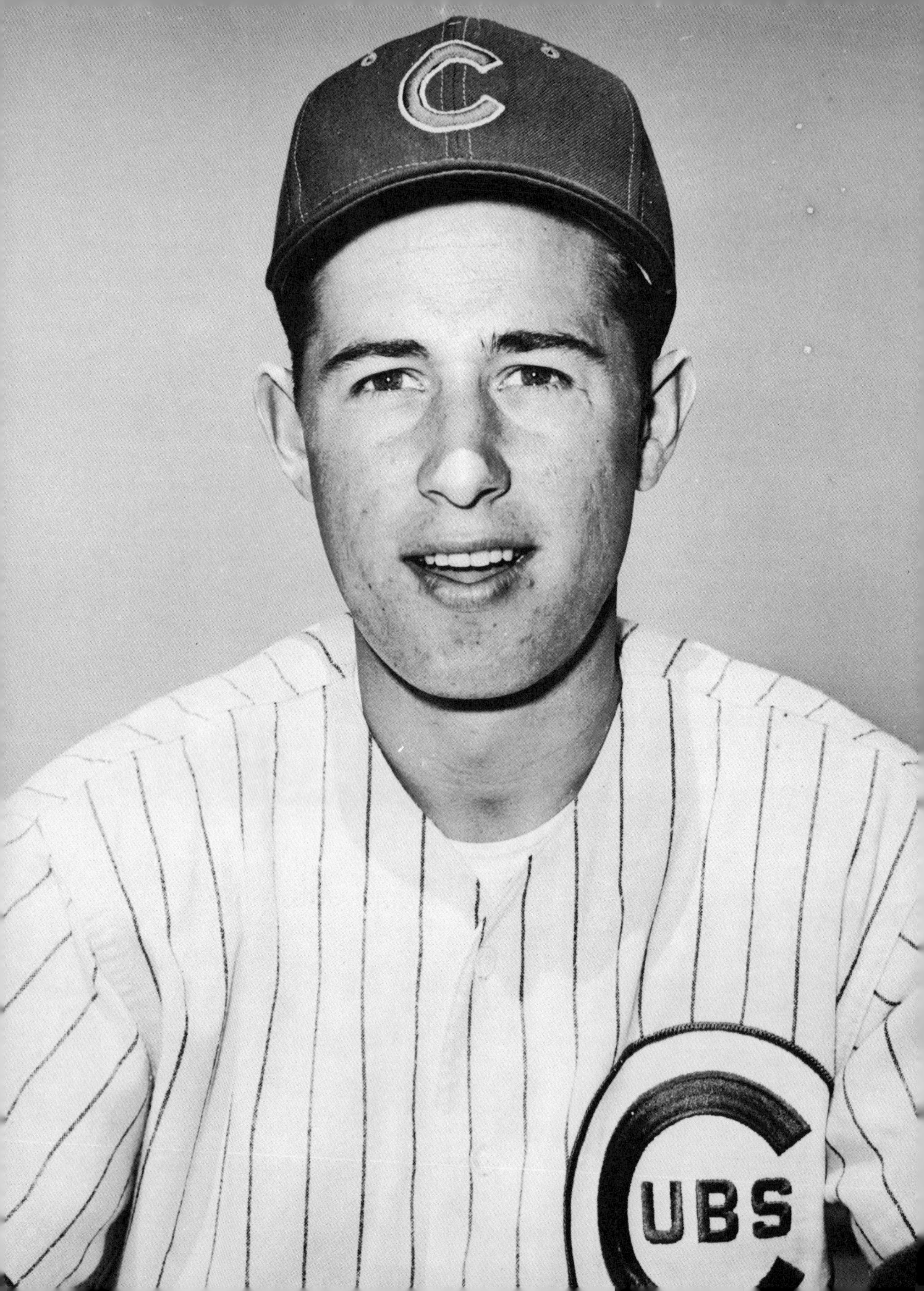
UBS

In 1946, the Cubs held on for third place in the league. In 1978, they were third in the N.L. Eastern Division, which was created in 1969.

But the Cubs most memorable pennant challenges since 1945 came in a solid six-year period. From 1967 to 1972, Chicago recorded three second place finishes and three thirds. The closest finish of those races came in 1969. It looked as if the Cubs had the National League title wrapped up. But the New York Mets — who would become known as "The Amazin' Mets" — put on a furious late charge to win the pennant and the Series.

Even though Chicago hasn't won another pennant yet, some great baseball players have passed through the Cubs' clubhouse.

•There was Billy Williams, who came to the club in 1959. He played in 1,117 consecutive games for the Cubs, from September 22, 1963, to September 3, 1970.

Williams batted .333 in 1972 and narrowly lost the league's most valuable player award to Johnny Bench, even though Bench batted just .270. Billy was named most valuable player of the year by *The Sporting News*.

•There was Ron Santo, who joined Chicago on June 26, 1960. He was exausted from jet lag when he got into his first Cubs doubleheader, but he went 3-for-7 at the plate and batted in five runs. In 1966, Santo set the team record for longest consecutive-game hitting streak at 28 games.

•There was pitcher Ken Holtzman, who won 11 games in his first year with Chicago. The next season, he spent weekdays as a soldier in the armed forces reserves, and weekends pitching for the Cubs — and won all nine of his games!

Holtzman pitched two no-hitters for the Cubs. The first one came on August 19, 1969, with a 3-0 win against the Atlanta Braves. The second, on June 3, 1971,

BUT NONE TOUCHED HOME Chicago pitcher Rick Reuschel allowed three doubles and nine singles in a game on June 20, 1974 against the Pittsburgh Pirates. But none of those base runners crossed home plate, and Reuschel walked away with a 3-0 shutout.

The sure hands of infielder Ron Santo provided some memorable moments in the comeback years of the early 1960's.

THE LIP
Leo "The Lip" Durocher took over as Chicago manager in 1966. He was at the helm when the Cubs took second place three times and third three times from 1967 to 1972.

was a 1-0 victory over the Cincinnati Reds.

• There was relief pitcher Bruce Sutter, who set a National League record for saves with 37 in 1979.

• There was hurler Ferguson Jenkins, who arrived in 1966 and promptly held the Los Angeles Dodgers scoreless for more than five innings for his first victory, a 2-0 shutout. The next season, Fergie won 20 games. He set two club records for strikeouts: 274 for a single season, and 1,808 for a career.

But there was one Chicago player who was even more special than these superstars. He played for the Cubs from 1953 to 1971. Like other Cubs since 1945, he was never able to earn one of those precious World Series championship rings. But it didn't take away from the glitter of his stardom one bit.

MR. CUB

His father said Ernie Banks was the smallest baby he had ever seen. Ernie weighed only 5 pounds, 2 ounces at birth, but he grew into one of baseball's best players ever.

It was Banks' optimistic approach to baseball and life that earned him a unique nickname: "Mr. Cub".

Ernie grew up playing more softball than baseball. It didn't take him too long to adjust to the faster game, however. He played for the Kansas City Monarchs in the Negro Leagues, and jumped directly to the Cubs — never playing an inning of minor-league ball.

On the field, Banks did whatever the Cubs asked him to do — and he did it well. In 1959, he recorded a .985 fielding percentage as Chicago's shortstop. His specialty was handling those low grounders that had to be scooped out of the dirt. In 1969, Ernie's fielding mark was .997 as first baseman.

Banks did even more damage to the opposition when he stepped to the plate. He belted 512 home runs in his

All-Star delivery. The Cubs' ace reliever, Bruce Sutter, delivers a whistler in the eighth inning of the 1980 All-Star game.

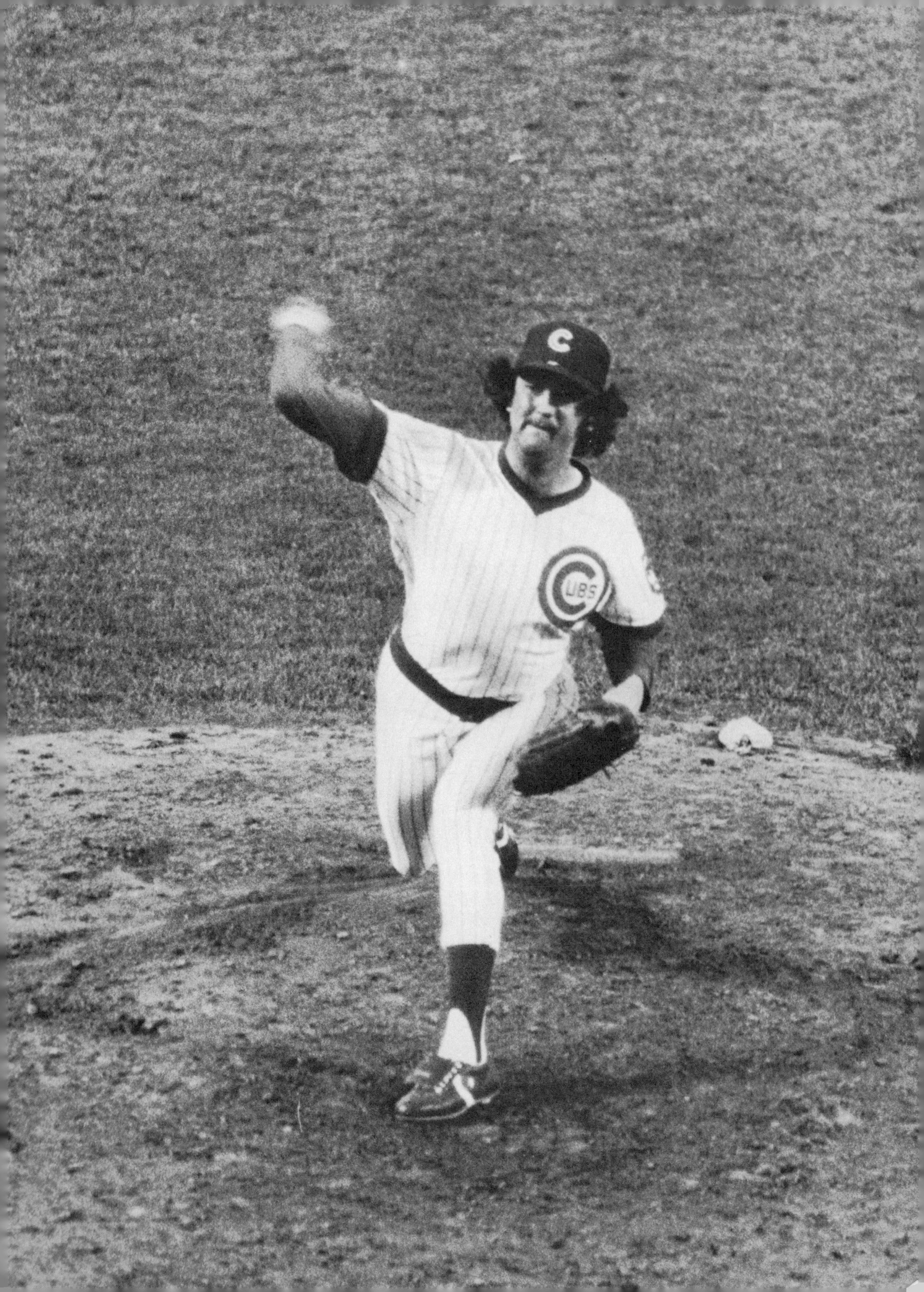
CUBS

44

career. In five separate seasons he hit 40 or more round-trippers. He won two home-run titles, two RBI crowns and two awards as the league's most valuable player.

No matter how glum the Cubs' situation seemed, Banks would see the bright side. He loved baseball, Wrigley Field and the Chicago fans. He was a complete team player. He acted like a winner, whether the Cubs were in last place or first. And he never neglected Chicago's fans, especially the younger ones.

Once Ernie was visiting a friend's home when the word got out that the famous Ernie Banks was in the neighborhood. Soon, dozens of kids were lined up in the front yard, waiting to catch a glimpse of their hero — and maybe get his autograph.

Ernie's friend saw the crowd and said, "We can leave through the kitchen door and get away." But Banks said, "Naw, we can't do that to all those kids." He stepped out the front door. The crowd roared its approval. And Ernie Banks stayed until every autograph had been signed.

Banks loved to tease his teammates. Sometimes they couldn't tell if he was pulling their leg or not. So when they weren't calling him "Mr. Cub", they'd usually call him "Uncle Josh".

Banks retired from the Cubs after the 1971 season. Even before then, in 1969, Chicago's fans voted him the greatest Cub of all time.

THE FUTURE LOOKS PROMISING

For 66 years, the Cubs were under the influence of the Wrigley Family. That ended in 1981, when the team was sold to the Chicago Tribune Company. The newspaper organization paid $20.5 million to buy the team.

Now it's a new era for the Cubs. For 1982, the Cubs' management brought in several people from the Phila-

"Mr. Cub." During the 1950's, Ernie Banks glued the team together with his awesome batting, near-perfect fielding and positive attitude.

RECORD HOARDER
Ernie Banks still holds eight career Cubs records: games played (2,528), at-bats (9,421), hits (2,583), doubles (407), home runs (512), total bases (4,706), runs batted in (1,636) and extra-base hits (1,009). He also holds the Cubs' record for single-season grand slam home runs: 5.

GOLD GLOVES Seven Cubs have been awarded Gold Glove Awards for their fielding talents: third baseman Ron Santo (5), Ernie Banks (one as shortstop, one as first baseman), shortstop Don Kessinger (2), second basemen Ken Hubbs and Glenn Beckert, pitcher Larry Jackson and catcher Randy Hundley.

delphia Phillies organization. Foremost is Dallas Green, who managed the Phillies when they won their World Series title. Green hired Lee Elia as manager, and brought along pitchers Dickie Noles and Dan Larson, plus three key players: veteran shortstop Larry Bowa, versatile catcher Keith Moreland, and popular third baseman Ryne Sandberg. Chicago's regulars were there, too: Second baseman Bump Wills, first baseman Bill Buckner, right fielder Leon Durham, pitcher Ken Kravec and free-agent reliever Bill Campbell, to name a few.

The last time the Chicago Cubs changed owners, it took the team only three years to win a National League pennant. Cub fans are hoping that 1984 or '85 will be their year again.

It's been a long, dry spell for the oldest professional baseball team in America. But along the way, they've won more games — over 8,000 — than any other team.

One thing is for certain: Win or lose, rain or shine, the team and its fans will always be together, working for their place at the top. That's what makes the Chicago Cubs so very special.

Fergie Jenkins showed the form that mowed down dozens of batters in the early 1970's.

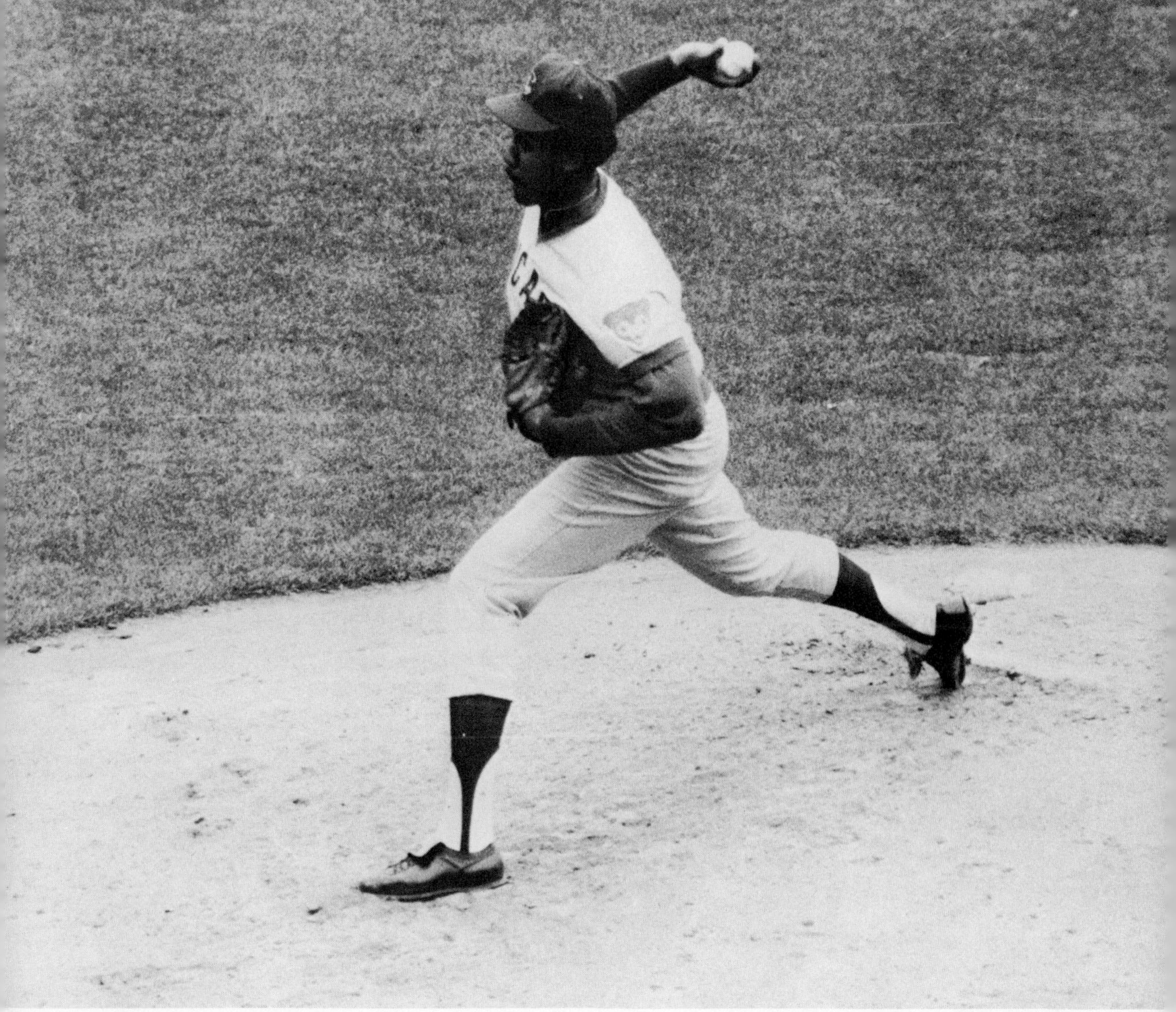

Infielder Don Kessinger rallied the Cubs in the gloomy hours of the mid-1970's. The 1980's look brighter.